A COURSE IN FOOTBALL FOR PLAYERS AND COACHES

A reprint of the 1912 Glenn S. "Pop" Warner classic

Carlisle, Pennsylvania

All new material copyright 2007 Tuxedo Press

Published by Tuxedo Press
Carlisle, PA 17015
LoneStarDietz.com

All rights reserved. No part of this publication may be reproduced, stored in a retrieval system, or transmitted, in any form or by any means, electronic, mechanical, photocopying, recording, or otherwise, without the prior permission of Tuxedo Press.

ISBN-10 0-9774486-6-5
ISBN-13 978-0-9774486-6-1
Library of Congress Control Number: 2007902237

GLENN S. WARNER

CONTENTS.

	PAGE
How Players Should be Outfitted	1–7
How to Train and How to Treat and Protect Injuries	8–13
How to Make and Use Tackling Apparatus and Charging Sleds	14–19
Tackling	20–24
Falling on the Ball	25–27
Blocking and Interfering	28–30
Punting	31–34
Forward Passing	35–37
Judging and Catching Punts	38–41
Place Kicking	42–43
Goal Kicking after Touchdown	44–46
Kick Off	46
Drop Kicking	47–49
How to Play End	50–54
How to Play Tackle	55–57
How to Play the Position of Guard	58–61
How to Play Center	62–64
How to Play Quarter-back	65–69
How to Play Half-back and Full-back	70–73
Football Practice	74–79
System of Signals	80–83
Generalship	84–90
Offense	91–135
Defense	136–143

PREFACE.

THE plan of teaching football by mail was suggested to me several years ago by the fact that there seemed to be no means available by which a student of the game could obtain instruction except by putting himself under the supervision of professional coaches upon the field of play. This situation has come about by reason of the fact that no one of late years has had the courage to get out a book on the game, because changes in the rules have been so frequent and so radical that a book dealing with football would be out of date after one or two seasons, and therefore every team and every coach have had to work out their own systems of playing independent of any help from such sources.

There appeared to be a great demand for an inexpensive means of learning the fine points of the game, and in 1908 I inaugurated the plan of teaching football by means of a complete and comprehensive correspondence course.

The results during the past four seasons have been so uniformly satisfactory to those who have had the course that I have been encouraged to revise it in accordance with the new rules and publish it in book form, feeling assured that it will attain a much wider circulation (because published in a more handy and attractive form and at a fraction of its former price) and therefore be of more service in spreading information and knowledge of this most important and least understood branch of school and college sport.

The course has not been prepared for the general public but is strictly a text book for players and for those whose business or pleasure it may be to instruct players and teams.

GLENN S. WARNER.

How Players Should be Outfitted

THE outfitting of a football player or team is one of the most important things to consider. No player can make the most of his ability or efforts if he is poorly outfitted. This does not mean that his suit, padding and protectors must be expensive since, with the exception of shoes, a good outfit can consist of very inexpensive material and yet be durable, light weight, and afford ample protection.

The tendency from year to year has been to wear less padding and lighter suits, and since the change in the rules, which makes the game more open, less rough, and puts a premium upon speed, the need of heavy padding and cumbersome protectors has not been so great.

SHOES.

The most important part of a player's outfit is his shoes, since without good footing a player is greatly handicapped in almost everything he attempts to do; not only that, but cheap or illfitting shoes are likely to cause sprained ankles. The shoes should be strong but not too heavy, and they should be as broad across the ball of the foot and toes as the foot will stand, in order to provide plenty of room for the cleats, greater surface contact with the ground, and consequently a better foothold. This makes the shoes easier on the feet and the liability to sprained ankles by turning the foot side ways much less. Therefore by all means wear broad toed shoes.

Unless strong leather ankle supporters are worn the tops of the shoes should come well above the ankle so as to strengthen and support the ankle joints. Many players prefer to wear low top shoes over leather ankle supporters as this allows a little more freedom to the ankle joints; but a rather high top shoe tightly laced, often renders an ankle supporter unnecessary. The ankle joint gives football players more trouble than any other part of the body, and nearly all ankle sprains are caused by a side turn or twist of the foot. Broad soled shoes will save some ankles, leather ankle supporters will prevent a great many more, and high top shoes are an added protection, but experience has proved to my satisfaction that the steel Spalding ankle brace—invented by Mike Murphy, sewed into the shoe, almost wholly prevents side sprains of the ankle. Where these are in the shoes and the shoes are kept tightly laced, there need be no other ankle supporter worn, and the freedom of movement of the foot and ankle is not seriously interfered with.

The sole of the shoe should be just thick enough to provide a solid base for the cleats which should be, for ordinary use, at least a half inch long and so distributed over the sole of the shoe as not hurt the foot by pressing through the sole against it in spots. Care should be taken to have the cleats extend flush with the edges of the sole, to prevent turning the foot over. There should be three small cleats on the heel, or one long one extending clear across. The cleats for ordinary wear should be about three thicknesses of ordinary sole leather, nailed on with a row of nails driven in as close together as possible, and long enough so that they will clinch on the inside of the shoe. They should be trimmed down with a knife closely to the heads of the nails, and should not be too broad at the base.

One pair of shoes can easily be made to do for practice and for playing in the games on either dry or wet fields by changing the cleats to suit the conditions, but many players, where the expense can be afforded, have as many as three pairs of shoes; one rather heavy pair for practice, one light pair cleated for dry fields, and one light pair cleated with extra long cleats suitable for wet or muddy fields. For a dry field the cleats should not be too long. They should be rather closely distributed over the sole of the shoe and should be sharp. For wet or muddy fields the cleats should be much longer—four thicknesses of sole leather—and they should not be so numerous, because in that case the mud and dirt will stick between the cleats and make the shoe heavy and the cleats of little use. The illustration shows three styles of cleats —the first is about the best arrangement for dry fields and ordinary use and the other two are suited to wet or soft fields. When teams have been evenly matched I have known many games to be won on a wet field by reason of the fact that the players of the winning team were properly shod with wet weather cleats which gave them good solid footing, while the losing team wore ordinary cleats which clogged up with mud and were not long enough to cling to the ground.

If you use only one pair of shoes for all purposes it will pay you to have your shoemaker change the cleats from time to time to suit the condition of the ground on which you are to play.

STOCKINGS.

Stockings are not an important item in a player's outfit. They are worn to protect the foot from the shoes, to prevent abrasions of the skin on the shins, and to keep the lower part of the leg warm in cold weather. They can be of cotton or wool, but it is a mistake to have them very heavy because in warm weather they retain the perspiration and get heavy while in wet weather they act as a sponge, absorb the water, and thus slow up the player by reason of the increased and useless weight he has to carry. In the south where warm weather is common during the football season, and in other parts of the country on wet days, teams sometimes wear no stockings, but simply short socks which come to the tops of the shoes.

This is a wise plan, but where no stockings are worn the player should wear light shin guards.

PANTS.

Next to the shoes the trousers are the most important part of the suit. They should be made of canvas or kahki cloth. Canvas is the cheapest and at the same time the strongest and most universally used.

Trousers should not be so tight as to prevent perfect freedom of movement, nor should they be any more loose fitting and baggy than necessary, because the more loosely they fit the greater opportunity is afforded the opposing players for securing a firm hold in tackling, and the padding, especially at the knees, will more likely shift away from the spot it is designed to protect.

There should be light pads upon the hips, and most players depend upon pads sewed in the trousers to protect the knees. These pads can be of any light soft material but hair pads are the best, since they are lighter, do not pack so hard or so quickly as others, and they do not absorb and retain moisture. Many players prefer to have their knee pads separate from the pants and strapped directly to the knee. This is really the best plan, because the pads will stay in place and not shift about as they will when attached to the pants, and on occasions when no knee pads are needed, the trouble of ripping out and sewing in again, or of wearing another pair of unpadded pants is avoided. These pads are generally made of good wool felt about one half inch thick, large enough to amply cover the knee joint, and fastened on by means of a light strap which is attached to the bottom of the pad and buckled around the leg next to the skin just below the knee. The illustration shown under another heading gives you an idea of how they are made and worn. Anyone can easily make them. but such pads can be secured of A. G. Spalding and Bros.

Knee, hip, and other pads do not prevent sprained or wrenched joints but only help to prevent bruises, consequently they are not very important or necessary except to be worn in practice to protect those parts of the body which are continually coming in contact with the ground, with the opposing players, and which would gradually, by repeated contact, become sore and tender. Therefore it is wise to wear such pads during practice and in smaller games in order to protect every part of the body as much as possible. Late in the season when the fields are unusally soft and the player is toughened by weeks of practice, he can easily do without soft padding for the important games without taking much chance of any serious injury. Certainly no soft pads should be used in playing upon a wet field, since at such times, besides their being of practically no use, they take up the moisture and handicap the player greatly with useless weight.

The part of the body covered by the trousers which is the most liable to injury, and which is the hardest to protect, is the large muscle of the thigh. This is especially true of the backs or other players who carry the ball, since the thigh is the part which generally must bear the impact of collision with opponents who tackle them. It is therefore quite necessary that the thighs should be protected both in practice and in games, whether played on dry fields or not. Soft pads for this purpose, or quilted thighs in the trousers, are of no use and are little used. The cane strips so generally used, afford some protection and are better than nothing, but what is needed is a hard stiff protector conformed to the shape of the leg, covering the front and side of the thigh, and fastened to the trousers so that it will distribute any severe blow over the entire surface the protecter covers. Such protecters can be made either of aluminum, papier-mache, or fibre, padded so as to conform to the rules, and they should be as light as they can be made to do the work. Your hardware man can get sheet aluminum for you, or better still, you can get hard fibre just suited to your needs from the American Vulcanized Fibre Co., of Wilmington, Del. This fibre should be about .07 of an inch thick and after being softened by soaking in water and moulded into shape, it should be water-proofed by varnishing when dry, and incased in light oil cloth. The protectors can then be sewed into the legs of the trousers and will hold their shape and **give** the results desired. The above described thigh pads can now **be** secured, all made up, from Spalding and other leading athletic **out**fitters.

Many players are provided with one pair of well padded trousers for practice and the smaller games, and another light unpadded pair for use in the more important games, and it is always well to have an extra light dry pair to put on between halves on wet days.

JERSEYS

The jersey should be strong but not too heavy, and it should be padded at the elbows and shoulders, unless pads are used for the latter place separate from the jersey. Elbow pads save that joint many bruises and as they are light and do not handicap the player much, even when soaked with water, they are generally worn throughout the season. They can, however, easily be dispensed with late in the season without any material danger to the player.

In my opinion it is most important to protect the shoulders, not only in practice but in all the games on all kinds of fields, and in planning such protection it is well to consider the effect upon opponents which various pads will have, since it is with the shoulder that most of the tackling, charging, and blocking is done. It is obvious that soft pads on the shoulders will save the opponents from as many hard bumps as they will the man wearing them; therefore it seems that a hard pad, moulded and fitted to the shoulder, will not only distribute any hard blow over a large surface and protect the man wearing it, but it will present a hard convex surface to the opponents. Such pads can be procured from Spalding's, but they are a bit uncomfortable until they become conformed to the shoulder, and most players prefer the soft hair pads sewed on the jersey or worn separately under the jersey.

The jersey should be worn tucked inside the belt or supporter, because when it is worn outside the trousers it affords opponents a better chance to get a grasp upon the player when carrying the ball.

HEAD PROTECTORS

Many players do not care to wear head protectors of any kind as they interfere to some extent with the hearing, are warm, and add weight to the uniform. Others will not play without them as they claim a head protector gives them more confidence, saves their head from many hard jolts, and keeps their ears from becoming torn or sore. I do not encourage their use, nor do I object if the players I am coaching prefer to wear them. I have never seen an accident to the head which was serious, but I have many times seen cases when hard bumps on the head so dazed the players receivng them that they lost their memory for a time and had to be taken out of the game, and I believe that the men who carry the ball would do well to wear light head protectors to guard against such temporary injuries.

Good head protectors can be had at all prices, and in all grades from those made from the crown of an old felt hot with ear laps sewed on and connected under the chin by a strap, to the elaborate ones placed on the markets by the sporting goods firms, and one affords about the same protection as the other.

NOSE GUARDS

No player with any nerve at all wears a nose guard now-a-days unless he has a sore nose. They prevent clear vision, interfere with the breathing, add weight to carry around and provide very little protection. They should only be worn in cases where the nose is recovering from an injury.

SHIN GUARDS.

It is well to wear shin guards during practice or in games, in cases when the shin is sore.

Continued little bumps and barking of the shins in practice caused by other players heels when running in interference, or in other ways, are likely to inconvenience and annoy the players, and to prevent these, light shin guards should be worn in practice. In the games these little injuries will not be noticed, and the players quickly recover from them by protecting their shins until the next game.

SUPPORTERS

All players should wear a snug fitting supporter, and while there are many kinds to be had at all prices, the bike supporter seems to give the best satisfaction and most players wear it over their jersey, so as to prevent the latter from creeping up above the belt.

GENERAL HINTS

Make your outfit as light as possible to afford the protection needed.

If you have a sore or a weak spot wear special protection for that spot.

Some colors used in dyeing the stockings and jerseys are poisonous, and for this reason it is well to wear light white undershirts and stockings next the skin to prevent blood poisoning and boils. These should be washed once or twice a week.

Players often wear canvas jackets, in many cases connected to the trousers by means of elastic belts, making union suits. These jackets or union suits help to preserve the jerseys and make it a little harder for opponents to secure a hold upon the players wearing them, but they are too warm except in the coldest weather, prevent freedom of movement of the body and shoulders, make the suit heavier, and I have never thought them desirable. The tendency seems to be to wear them less and less each sason.

Tight fitting garters to hold up the stockings should not be worn, as these interfere with the proper circulation of the blood and often cause cramps. If it is necessary to wear them they should be made of good elastic and be at least an inch wide.

In outfitting teams I have coached in past years I have shopped around among different firms in order to determine where to buy supplies to the best advantage, and I have found that the goods of A. G. Spalding & Bros. generally give the best satisfaction, considering variety to select from, range of prices, and promptness of delivery. If you want what you want when you want it you can generally get it from Spaldings.

How to Train, and How to Treat and Protect Injuries.

RULES of training for football players are about the same as for any other branch of athletics where endurance, strength and quickness are required, but the game and the practice require such hard work that it is a waste of energy which might better be applied to learning the game to engage in such exercises as running around the track or the gridiron, calisthenics or setting up exercises. A player can get all the exercise he needs in practicing the rudiments of the game and engaging in the daily scrimmages. In cases where the player is kept out of all rough work and scrimmages on account of an injury he should of course take his exercise in any way he can which will not affect the injury, but as a general rule a player should confine his efforts to practicing something that will help him in the game.

When the football season starts, the players who are to try for the team present themselves in every kind of physical condition. Some may have been working at manual labor and start training in good physical condition; others may have loafed all summer and start practice overweight and soft; and still others may have been overdone during the hot season and find themselves underweight and run-down. All are anxious to make the team, and they start practice with a great deal of enthusiasn and determination.

It is a mistake very often made, even where there are supposed to be good trainers in charge, to start the training season with hard, rough work before the players have gradually worked up to such work. It is generally in the first two weeks of practice, when the players are full of ambition and determination, that they are most likely to overdo or get laid up with an injury which may keep them out of the game for the whole season. In my opinion the work for all the candidates should be about the same. The soft fat candidate will find light work hard for him and he will sweat and lose weight, but will gradually become able to do harder work. The thin overworked man needs the same light work to give him enough exercise to create a good appetite and make him sleep well, while the man who is already in good physical condition does not need more than the light practice the others are given. This work will be easy for him, and he will store up energy for use later in the season.

It would be unwise to work the soft fat man hard at the start with the idea of taking off weight and hardening him up. More likely he will strain himself or get disgusted with the game and quit. It would be a mistake to be too easy on the player who is under weight, as he needs a moderate amount of work. Therefore I am of the opinion that all sorts of candidates will thrive, and gradually train up or down according to their needs, or keep in condition on the same moderate amount of work, gradually increased from week to week, until they are in good condition, when care should be taken that they do not overdo and begin to lose their speed and aggressiveness.

When a player begins to lose interest in his work, and the practice becomes irksome and he hates to go to the field, it is time he took a day or two off before it is too late. He will find that with a rest of a day or two he will feel like getting into the game again, and he should be careful not to work too hard from that time on. The coach dislikes to have a player miss a day's practice and often makes the mistake of insisting upon daily attendance in cases where, by laying a man off a day or two days or a week, he would save a good man for usefulness to the team, whereas by working him when he shows signs of staleness the player is likely to be rendered useless for the balance of the season.

The same mistake is often made in handling a player who has suffered an injury, and too often his anxiety to get back into the game, and the coaches fear that he will miss too much practice, causes him to start rough work too soon, the injury is made worse, and he is laid up for a long time, whereas by the use of a little patience and caution he would remain out of practice long enough to recover from the injury, and suffer no ill effects from it when he started rough work again.

Players will often deceive their coaches or trainers and not mention an injury, or the fact that they are not feeling well, for fear that they will be laid off for a day or two and other players will get their places. The coach, not knowing that anything is wrong, will often misjudge a player who is unable to do his best work by reason of the injury, and it would be much better for the player and every one concerned if he would report all injuries or indisposition to the coach or trainer, so that he might be treated at once, and that the player, so handicapped, may not be sized up wrongly by those in charge.

So anxious are some players to get into a game that they will practice deception in this way and go into the game in no condition to play, and in such cases their playing is likely to be so inferior as to queer them for the rest of the season. This sort of deception is not fair to the coaches, the rest of the team, nor to the player himself.

This illustration shows hard shoulder and collar bone protectors of moulded fiber, lined inside and outside with felt,—an injured-rib protector of same material, felt lined only upon the inside,—bike supporter,—a muscle bruise protector made of fiber or alluminum, and padded around the edges with thick felt as shown by the one held in the hand,—and felt knee pads, described in "How players should be outfitted." The rib and muscle protectors are held in place by adhesive tape. More tape is usually needed than is shown in the cut.

It is needless to say that no player should use tobacco in any form, as its use seriously effects the wind and interferes with his doing his best work.

Stimulants of all kinds should be avoided, and the player should eat good but plain food at regular hours, and nothing should be eaten between meals. The heaviest meal should be in the evening and not too soon after practice.

A football player needs plenty of sleep and should get to bed by ten o'clock every night.

Under the heading "how players should be outfitted" it was explained how to so protect the parts most liable to injury so as to avoid injuries as far as possible, but in spite of all precautions accidents are likely to happen. Injuries which are serious enough to keep a player from practice should be intelligently treated, and patiently borne until recovery and, as explained above, the player should not be in too much of a hurry to jump into the game again.

Nature will cure all bruises and sprains but it requires time. In the case of bruises nature can be aided by the proper use of electricity, vibrating machines and massage; but these used to excess will retard the recovery, and therefore they should only be used by physicians or those who understand their use. Electricity and massage will also aid nature in curing sprains, while good linaments applied in connection with massage will add to its effectiveness.

If the bruise is not a bad one, but simply painful to a blow, for instance a bruised thigh muscle or "charley horse," a protector can be made which will prevent any hard blow from reaching the spot, and the the player can continue his practice. Such a protector should be in the nature of a bridge, made from a piece of aluminun or fiber large enough to more than cover the tender spot, shaped to the part to be covered, and resting around its edges upon a strip of half-inch felt, so that all the pressure or concussion from any hard blow will be distributed through the felt all around the sore spot but not on it. This protector should be held in place by strips of adhesive plaster. With a protector of this kind properly made and adjusted, a "charley horse" or muscle bruise need not keep any player out of the game or practice. Such protectors are very usuful in protecting boils and other painful spots, and are on the same principle as most cornpads, with the added protection of a cover or bridge which prevents anything from touching the injured part. The illustration on the preceding page shows how such a protector is made and applied.

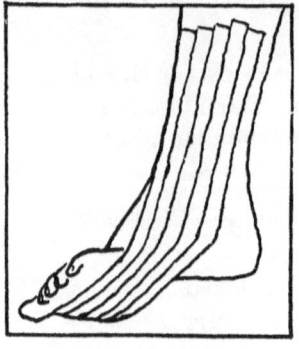 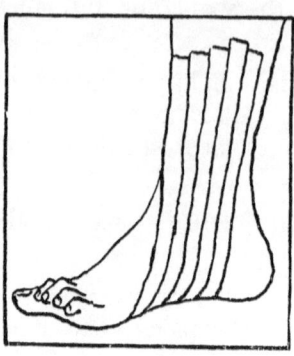 

For strapping the ankle, strips of adhesive plaster one and a half inches in width are required. The first strap is started about 5 inches above the ankle on the inner or outer side (according to which side is sprained) at the edge of the Tendon Achilles, and carried across the sole of the foot to the base of the great or little toe. Several of these straps are applied, covering the outer (or inner) side of the ankle. A strap is placed with its middle at the front of the heel, the ends being carried nearly to the toes, leaving about an inch of space between them. A number of these straps are applied, lapped over each other about a half inch, until the ankle joint is well covered. The straps should not quite meet in front. This bandage may be advantageously employed at any stage of the injury.

Adhesive plaster comes in very handy and is used a great deal by the leading teams both for holding pads and protectors in place and for wrapping, bracing, and strengthening sprained joints. A badly sprained ankle can often be so braced and strengthened by its use that the player can use the foot almost as well as before the sprain. Only in the most serious cases is it necessary for a player to stay out of an important game by reason of a sprained ankle. The illustration shows how the adhesive plaster or tape should be applied.

Broken or cracked ribs or a torn cartilage between the ribs should be protected by plates of fiber or aluminun, fitted to the body and held in place by adhesive tape as shown in the illustration on another page.

The knee is a hard joint to protect when sprained, but it can be strengthened and braced to a certain extent by the aid of an elastic bandage. In bad cases where the knee joint is weak and continually giving trouble, a hard fiber protector fitting half way around the leg above and below the knee, with a joint at the sides corresponding to the knee, padded and fastened in place by adhesive tape, will generally so brace any knee, that it will give little trouble. Such knee braces can be purchased from Spalding's and fitted to any knee.

The shoulders have to stand many hard knocks and unless they are properly protected they are likely to be injured. A rather frequent injury is the tearing of the ligaments which hold one of the bones in place at the point of the shoulder. This injury renders a small spot very tender to the touch and without protection a player having such an injury would be unable to use his shoulder at all. Such an injury should first be tightly strapped with adhesive tape, the tape coming well down on the chest and back and pulled tightly over the injured part in order to hold the bone in place and strengthen the injured ligaments; then by the same method, and in the same manner as explained previously, a protector can be made in the nature of a bridge, resting on felt placed around the injured part, and the whole fitted and held in place by means of adhesive plaster. The ordinary pad should be placed over this, and the shoulder can then be used and the injury will heal at the same time.

GENERAL HINTS

It is better to be undertrained than overtrained, because when undertrained the fault can be easily corrected by more and harder work, while overtraining is hard to correct and can only be remedied by rest, probably just at a time when the coach wants to get in some hard work to prepare for an important game.

If a player cannot do himself justice by reason of injuries, he should not get into the game until the handicap is removed.

A player of ordinary ability with a sound body will play better than a badly crippled star player, and the latter may come around in good shape for the next game if given a layoff.

A player should not start out at the beginning of practice at a faster pace than he can keep up throughout the season. Many players fairly tear up the ground with fierceness the first few days and then gradually get very tame as the season progresses.

Worrying is the most useless and at the same time the hardest work an athlete can do.

How to Make and Use Tackling Apparatus and Charging Sleds

EVERY team should have a tackling bag or dummy to aid in developing this most important department of the game, because a great deal of this practice is necessary, and tackling each other hard, if practiced sufficiently to make the team proficient, would be unnecessarily severe upon the players. Some tackling of each other for practice should be indulged in, but the main dependence in developing good tacklers should be the tackling bag or dummy. This can be so simple and so inexpensive that no team need be without one.

The simplest form of tackling bag consists of a grain sack, filled with saw dust and suspended from the limb of a tree, as shown in the first drawing. The bag should be far enough away from the trunk of the tree to enable it to swing freely in any direction, and to enable the players to tackle without danger of hitting the tree. The higher the limb from which the bag is suspended the better, as a longer swing can be secured when the bag is suspended from a high point. The bag should be hung so that its bottom will be just off the ground. If unable to procure a grain sack of the right proportions, a better bag can be made out of heavy white duck or canvas. It should be about four feet long and as large around as a man's body.

A tackling bag which will come down when tackled, somewhat as a player will fall, is shown in the second drawing. It is suspended by a rope which passes through two pulleys, and is attached to a weight made by about half filling a grain sack with sand or dirt. The whole should be so adjusted that the weight, when resting upon the ground, will just hold the tackling bag off the ground. When tackled, the tackler's weight added to that of the bag, will raise the weight up and let the bag down. When released, the weight brings the bag again into position.

If no tree is handy, the third drawing shows how a still more elaborate tackling machine can be made. The dummy can be made or purchased, or a bag similar to those shown in the other drawings will answer the purpose.

Simplest form of tackling bag.

An inexpensive tackling bag which can be thrown to the ground when tackled.

Two timbers 4 x 4 inches square and about 9 or 10 feet long, should be planted in the ground about 1 foot deep and about 30 feet apart, and held upright by guy ropes fastened to stakes driven into the ground. A three-quarter inch rope should be fastened to the upper end of one of the uprights and run through a pulley attached to the end of the other, and then down to a weight, made as explained previously. The dummy, or bag, is suspended by a rope attached to a pulley, which runs upon the rope connecting the two uprights. It should hang about one or two inches from the ground. A smaller rope is attached to the pulley and runs through smaller pulleys attached to each upright. This is for the purpose of pulling the dummy back and forth between the posts to imitate a man running. This tackling arrangement is about the best that can be devised for tackling practice. The dummy with the patent release, allowing it to become unfastened when tackled, is very good, but too much time has to be consumed in hanging it up again after each tackle.

In using these tackling bags or dummies, they can be swung or pulled back and forth in front of the tacklers to give them practice in tackling from the side, or directly toward or away from them to give them practice in tackling head-on or from the rear. When tackling from the side, the player should not use his shoulder, but should shoot his body across the path of the dummy, as shown in the 2nd drawing. The third drawing gives a rear view of this side tackle, and shows how the hands should be locked by grasping the wrist with the other hand. The players should be given practice in tackling the dummy or player passing from right to left, and vice versa, until they can tackle on either side with equal ease.

The first drawing shows a player meeting the dummy coming directly toward him. Such tackles should be made with the shoulder, and the dummy should be forced backward to the ground with the tackler on top.

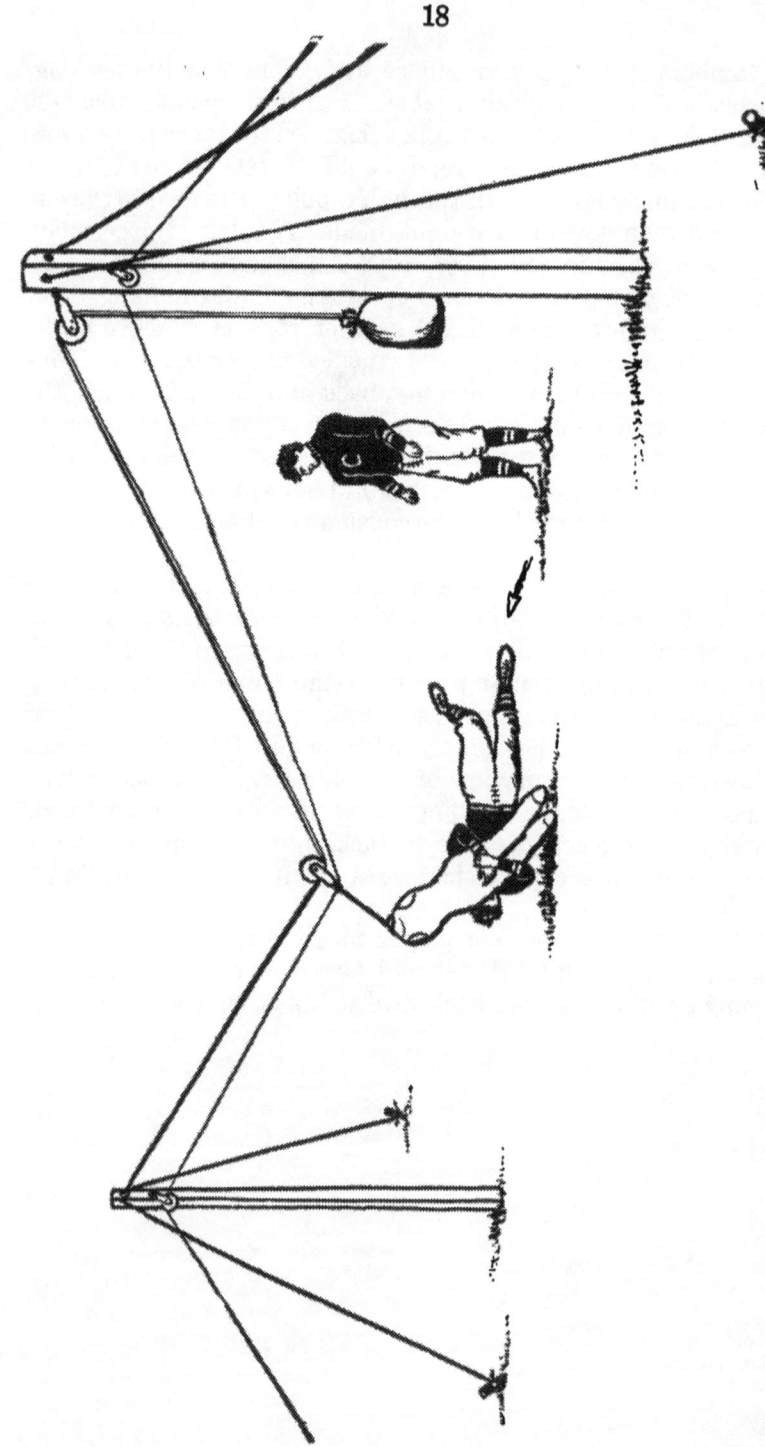

The best form of tackling dummy. It can be pulled back and forth to imitate a man running, and can be thrown when tackled.

HOW TO MAKE AND USE A CHARGING SLED.

A charging sled aids greatly in developing the players in hard, quick charging and pushing, although it is not quite as necessary as a tackling dummy. The sled should be heavy enough to stand hard usage and make it rather difficult for the players to shove it along. There should be three runners made from timbers eight inches square and about seven or eight feet long—one at each end and one in the center. The sled should be about sixteen feet across, and the padded board, against which the players charge, should be two and one-half feet from the ground to its upper edge. The players must be taught to charge low. Nearly all the charging sleds I have seen have been too high. This charging surface should be about ten inches wide, and padded heavily with anything that will form a cushion for the shoulder when the charge is made. The three runners should be rounded upon the opposite end from the charging board, so that the sled will slide along the ground evenly, and not tear up the sod. The whole machine should be made of heavy timbers and well braced, as it must stand hard usage and is all the more valuable if fairly heavy. If it pushes along too easily, it can be weighted down with one or two players. In using the charging sled, the players should line up exactly as they would against the opposing line, and the same distance away. The center can be the middle man, and the signal can be his snap of the ball, as in a regular scrimmage. If a starting signal is used, this can be used to advantage in practicing charging. After the charge is made, the players should continue to push the sled about five yards. This will teach them to remain close to the ground when charging, and will develop their backs and legs.

An improvement upon the above illustrated and described charging sled could be made in the following manner. Instead of the horizontal padded timber which extends the length of the sled, upright padded timbers one foot wide and two and a half feet high, placed in a vertical position so as to represent individual opponents, and about two and a half feet apart, would give better practice because such individual padded posts would allow the heads of the players to pass by them and the padded surfaces to be met by the shoulders squarely, exactly as if they were opposing players. There should be seven of these padded uprights to each sled, so as to accommodate a full line from end to end.

Tackling.

NO player should hope to be placed upon a team unless he is a good tackler. This is one of the most important rudiments of the game which every player should thoroughly master. It tests a player's nerve more than anything else he has to do, and a sure, fearless tackler is valuable to any team, no matter what his other qualifications may be. Innumerable games have been lost by reason of a missed tackle, and any number of defeats have been prevented by a well executed tackle of an opponent speeding toward the coveted goal.

There are many good features about a football game that the majority of spectators do not see or appreciate, but a tackle or a missed tackle is always seen by nearly every one on the field, since the spectators are watching the man carrying the ball, and are sure to note all the attempts to stop his progress, whether successful or not.

This drawing shows the correct form of tackling with the shoulder when the runner can be met directly in front. The tackler has gone under the stiff-arm of the runner, and the latter's momentum has carried him off the ground. The finish is shown upon the next page.

A small player is often able to beat out his heavier competitors for a place on the team because of his sure tackling, when as a matter of fact there is no reason why a small man should tackle any better than a large one. The reason so many small men do tackle better is simply because, on account of their size, they are forced to tackle low and hard in order to bring down their heavier opponents, whereas a big man too often depends more upon his size and strength than upon correct form in tackling.

Practice, head-work, and nerve, are necessary in acquiring ability in this important feature of football.

Practice can be had by tackling the dummy of a tackling machine, a stuffed bag suspended from the limb of a tree, or by tackling other players. The practice should not be hard at first, especially when tackling other players, and special attention should be devoted to good form. It is necessary to crouch low and then shoot the body forward, close to the ground, and in a horizontal position to it, by a powerful leg drive. The low crouch and hard leg drive, are necessary to get under and break down the stiff arm of the man who will try to ward off the tackler.

Different methods of tackling should be used for different situations, and these should be practiced and mastered thoroughly. For instance, a man coming straight at a tackler should be met squarely with the shoulder just above the knees. The tackler should drive his body forward by straightening his legs, keeping his feet on the ground, his straight body and leg presenting a solid brace which the momentum of the oncoming player cannot topple over. If correctly met, the momentum of the man tackled, thus meeting a solid brace, will lift him off his feet, and the tackler can carry him back to the ground with his shoulder in the pit of his stomach in no gentle manner as shown in the illustration on the preceding page.

While this is the ideal way to meet an oncoming man with the ball, it more often happens that the runner will try to pass to the side of the tackler, and therefore a player should be able to tackle with equal

This shows a player tackling from the side. He has forced the man carrying the ball to try to pass him upon the side upon which the ball is held, making it impossible for the runner to use his free arm in warding off the tackler. Note how far the body extends across the path of the runner, and how the hands are locked.

ease, a runner passing either to the right or left of him. The correct method of tackling in such cases is not to depend upon the shoulder, but more upon the body. The player should shoot his body across the path of the runner, grasping both legs and pinning them tightly to his breast. It is well to dive farther than it seems necessary, because the runner may partly hold the tackler back by his free arm and at the same time try to get his legs farther away from him, but of course he should be careful to have one foot upon the ground when the runner is met. If he tackles from the side by the shoulder, unless he knocks the runner over, the tackler will only have his arms to stop him with, and often the runner can free himself and continue his course. Some players have the fault of grasping one leg in each arm, while the correct method is to pin both legs firmly together with the arms securely locked.

In practicing tackling, the player should tackle from both sides, straight ahead, and from behind, using both the dummy and other players for this purpose, and some practice should be indulged in every day until after the middle of the season.

Head-work, or the use of brains and judgment in tackling, is a very important consideration. The man carrying the ball has one arm free, and he probably is expert in using this free arm in warding off tacklers; therefore the tackler should remember that the runner will try to pass him upon the side on which he has his free arm. It should be the aim of the tackler to so maneuver for position, as to compel the runner to try to pass him on the side where his free arm will be of little use. The runner will also use his head, and will try to make the tackler think he is going that way anyway, and endeavor to deceive him by dodging. He may also shift the ball to the other arm just before reaching the tackler. All these things should be watched, for generally a tackler can force the runner to try to pass him on the side he wishes.

The illustrations show correct methods of tackling and should be closely studied.

POINTERS

A tackler should remember that as a rule, a hard tackle hurts the opponent more than it does the tackler, and when met fiercely a few times, a runner is inclined to slow up and try to save himself. On the other hand if the tackler shows signs of fear or weakness, the runner will come at him more fiercely each time.

In practicing tackling, it is well to keep the hands closed so as to learn to depend upon the body and arms. It is too often the case that tacklers depend upon securing a grasp upon the runner's clothes or legs with their hands.

Nine times out of ten a tackler, who runs up to the runner and attempts to grab him without using the low crouch and hard leg drive will be warded off by the stiff arm. The low crouch and the hard leg drive are necessary to enable the tackler to get under or break down the runner's guard.

Tackling is a knack easily acquired by some players and difficult to learn by others, but when once learned it is never forgotten.

No team can make many long runs, or run up a large score against a team whose players are all good tacklers and nervy, no matter how much they may be out-classed.

Falling on the Ball.

THE more open game, now made necessary by the changed rules, especially the change requiring ten yards to be gained in a certain number of downs, instead of five yards, has put a premium upon taking chances, and consequently the ball is fumbled a great deal more than it used to be when the rules encouraged conservatism, and when only those plays were used in which there was little chance of a fumble.

There are ten chances now to recover fumbles where there was one a few years ago, and consequently it is much more necessary to know how to fall on the ball and recover fumbles than formerly.

A player should be able to drop on the ball on either side, make running dives for it, and become accustomed to securing it under all sorts of conditions and circumstances.

Most players become accustomed to dropping on the ball on one side, and as that is the easier, and they can do better that way, they never practice dropping on it with the other side. If a player can fall on the ball one way he should confine his efforts to learning to do it equally well by using the other side. Most players like to practice the things they can do well, but they should devote more time to those features of the game in which they are weak.

In falling on the ball the form to be followed is much the same as that used in tackling from the side. The player starts with his body

Drawing from snap shot of a famous player, showing the body near the ground in the act of springing forward to fall on the ball. His position also shows good form preparatory to a tackle just before the runner is met.

near the ground, gets in a good leg drive which shoots his body forward close to, and parallel with, the ground. He should land upon his side or hip, at the same time dropping the forearm of the side nearest the ground over the ball, and scooping it into a sort of pocket formed by his arms, his stomach or body, and his thighs. The player should not

This picture shows the body shooting through the air close to the ground, the right fore-arm in position to drop over the ball, and the left ready to aid in scooping the ball into the pocket formed by the arms, body and thighs.

fall *on* the ball but rather around it, and he should not go after it with his hands, as many do when they first start practice. As mentioned above, the player should be able to drop on either side equally well. The ball should be covered as much as possible when the opponents are close at hand, so that none of them can get it away from the man falling upon it, nor get their hands upon it in such a way that the referee may think it belongs to them. If none of the opponents are near enough to prevent the player gaining some ground after securing the ball, he should get to his feet as quickly as possible. Therefore it is advisable for the player to practice falling on the ball and rolling upon his feet. Practice will soon enable him to do this in remarkably quick time.

When an opponent is also endeavoring to fall on the ball, the player should throw himself between the opponent and the ball, and block him

Illustrating how the ball should be covered at the finish of falling on the ball.

off with his back, as shown in the illustration upon the next page. If they are both running in the same direction after the ball, the blocking can be done before the dive for the ball is made.

In these days of forward passes and other intricate plays the ball is often on the move, either rolling on the ground or bounding, and good judgment should be used as to when to try to grasp the ball, or pick it up without leaving the feet, and when to fall upon it. If the ball bounds so the player can grasp it while in the air, it is always wise to do so, but as a general rule when the ball is upon the ground it should be secured by falling upon it. There are times, of course, when the opponents are not near, and when the ball may wisely be picked up for a long run, but these instances are the exception.

The illustrations show quite well the correct form to be used in falling on the ball.

Blocking and Interfering.

In blocking and interfering there are three methods used by the best players, and all players should practice and make use of them. The best known method, and the one most commonly used, is the shoulder block. The form used in shoulder blocking is much the same as that used in tackling a player coming directly toward the tackler, except that in blocking. the hands and arms cannot be used. There is always a great temptation to use the arms, especially the elbows, and more penalties are probably suffered by reason of illegal use of the arms in connection with the shoulder block than from any other cause. For this reason this method of blocking or interfering, while the most generally used, is not so effective nor as good as the body block.

The body block is made by stooping over, hurling the body across the path of an opponent, and catching him above the knee with the side or hip as shown in the second illustration. This method of blocking, combined with the leg block, is the surest and best. If the player fails to catch the opponent on the hip he can quickly turn farther over and throw up one leg, in this way presenting a blocking surface six feet wide, whereas with the shoulder block the player only covers a space equal to the width of his shoulders, or about two feet, and at the same time is tempted to use his hands or arms. With the body and leg block there is no chance of suffering a penalty, and the opponents cannot so easily ward off the block with their hands, or side-step it.

This method of blocking can be used to advantage, not only in interfering for a runner, but by the line men in preventing their opponents from breaking through. The end especially, can use this body and leg block in blocking the opposing tackle on runs around his end. It is also valuable in blocking the opposing end from running down the field under punts

While there is a rule against holding and the use of hands and arms by the players of the side having possession of the ball, there is no rule against using the legs, and some players have been able to so develop their use that they can hold with their legs almost as effectively as with their arms, and even tackle with them.

There is always a temptation for the interferer, when blocking, to keep his feet, with the idea that he can put his man out of the way, and then block off other opponents. When he attempts to do this, the chances are that he will not get the first man out of the play, and he

will continue on only to hear the whistle, look around, and find the runner in the grasp of the man it was his primary business to take care of. It is better to put one dangerous man out of the play, even if the person doing it is put out also, than to only half block two or three.

The three snap shots upon the opposite page illustrate the three methods of blocking or interfering, and show how all may be used in connection with each other. In the first picture the interferer is blocking with his shoulder. If he was depending upon his shoulder entirely he should have his head on the opposite side of his opponent, but the second picture shows him using his body, and as his opponent works his way toward the path of the runner, the interferer turns his body, throws up his leg and blocks the opponent as shown in the third illustration.

This drawing shows how to hold the ball correctly, and the stiff-arm in position to ward off a tackler. It also shows correct form of the tackler, about to duck under the stiff-arm and tackle the runner low.

Punting

ALMOST any player can acquire accuracy and fairly good distance in punting by practice and the study of form. Care should be taken early in the season that too much practice should not be

Dropping the ball for a punt. Note how the hands are spread away from it so that it will drop true. The player has held the ball a bit too high.

indulged in, as the leg is liable to become sore and lame for the same reason that a baseball player's arm so often goes wrong, and it is no easy matter to get it into shape again when straining or overdoing has once got in its work.

The spiral punt is the one now most universally used because a ball punted in this way goes farther, can with practice be punted just as accurately, and is much harder to catch. In order to get the necessary distance and punt the spiral with accuracy, some practice should be devoted to it every day and great attention should be paid to form. It is correct form to hold the ball as far away from the body as possible, directly in front of the kicking foot, with one hand on each side of it

A noted expert just meeting the ball with the foot in the act of punting. The ball has dropped true and just fits the curve of the instep and the top of his foot. Note how he is getting his weight into the punt by leaning backward.

and the outer point of the ball slightly lower than the end nearest the body, at the same time taking a short step forward with the kicking foot. Then take a regular step with the other foot, drop the ball so that it will fall without turning, and meet it with the instep of the kicking foot about two and one-half feet from the ground. The foot should be extended and the leg should swing mostly from the hip and little at the knee. The punt should be followed out with the leg as far as possible and the body should bend backward so as to get the full weight of the player into the kick. The foot should meet the ball very slightly on the inside of it, and at the moment of contact the foot should be swung a little to the inside—the spiral twist of the ball being imparted in this manner.

In punting from behind the line of scrimmage, the punter should regulate the distance he stands to receive the ball from the center according to the time he takes in getting off his punts, and the ability of

The finish of the punt, showing how it has been followed out with the foot.

his team to prevent the opponents from getting to him. The ordinary distance is about eight to ten yards. If the punter can add five yards to his punt by receiving the ball two or three yards farther back and taking more time, it will pay to do it, as he not only gains two or three yards by so doing, but gives his line men more time to get down the field.

The punter should try to place his punt as far away from the best handler of punts in the back field as possible, and as soon as the ball leaves his foot he should always yell out—"Right," "Left," or "Short" according to the direction or distance the ball is traveling, in order that the ends and other line men may be quickly directed toward the spot the ball is likely to land.

The punter should regulate the distance of his punts by the speed of his ends in getting down the field to cover them, as it does not pay to punt beyond the point the ends can reach in time to tackle the runner as soon as he catches the ball.

The velocity and direction of the wind should also be taken into consideration. If punting with the wind, the ball should be sent up higher into the air as this will enable the wind to carry it farther down the field, and as it will be in the air longer, the ends will have more time to get down under it. The ball should be driven low and hard against the wind, as this is the only way much distance can be secured under such conditions.

A careful study of the illustrations will give valuable pointers in regard to correct form used by the best punters.

For quick punts from the ordinary scrimmage formation, the punt is often made from the side, and generally in punting from the side no atempt is made to use the spiral.

Forward Passing.

THE changes in the rules in recent years have made the forward pass an important feature of football. Under the rules which were in vogue prior to 1906 there was no passing or throwing the ball for distances of more than ten yards and therefore no necessity

Mt. Pleasant about to make a long pass.

for developing distance passing. The game as now played, however, requires at least two players of each team who can pass or throw the ball accurately for long distances, since the rules now place no restriction upon how far the ball may be passed in any direction.

In order to secure distance and accuracy there can be no question but that the ball should be thrown, instead of being passed with a stiff arm swung from the shoulder, and as in punting, better results can be obtained by the spiral.

Any player can develop the spiral throw by practice. Almost every player in the Indian squad learned how to throw the ball in this

The ball just leaving the hand on a forward pass.

way in a single season, many of them for distances of thirty-five and forty yards.

The ball should be held near the end, between the thumb and fingers as shown in the photograph illustrating the start of the pass. The throw should be made from above the shoulder, and during the throw the palm of the hand should always be upward and the long axis of the ball pointed in the direction the ball is to be thrown. This is done by slightly turning the hand as the arm moves forward. The spiral movement is imparted to the ball by letting it roll off the fingers at the finish of the throw.

This pass will become easy for any player after a little practice and study, and when acquired, will be found to be the best form of pass for all distances over five yards.

Finish of the spiral forward pass.

The player should practice making the pass after a run of five or ten yards either to the right or to the left, as a run to either side is usually necessary preliminary to the pass, in order that the players who may receive the pass may have more time to get into position and also to deceive the opponents into a belief that a run is being attempted instead of a forward pass.

Judging and Catching Punts

In judging punts, the catcher should always have in mind the direction and velocity of the wind and the effect it will have upon the ball. He should regulate the distance he stands from the punter in accordance with this, together with the ability of the punter. These things need not be gone into fully, because any player of good common sense should have them always in mind, and govern himself accordingly.

There is another thing, however, to consider in judging punts which few players take into consideration, and a thorough understanding of which will aid them greatly. This is the effect which the resistonce of the air has upon the course the ball will follow, and especially its effect upon spiral punts.

There are two kinds of spirals commonly punted—one where the long axis upon which the ball revolves maintains the same relative position with regard to the ground throughout its course, and the other where this axis gradually varies its position and follows the course of the ball, keeping its front end always pointed in the direction it is going like the head of an arrow. If the ball was round, the position of the axis on which it revolves would effect its course very little, but a football, being round one way and elliptical the other, the effect of the assistance of the air has a very marked influence upon its course, according to the position the ball maintains while traveling through the air.

It is obvious that the air resistance which the ball has to contend with, is greater when the ball is traveling with its side or largest surface exposed to the air in its path, than it is when the ball keeps its end continually pointed in the direction of its course, because in the latter less surface is presented to the air, and consequently the ball will travel faster and farther.

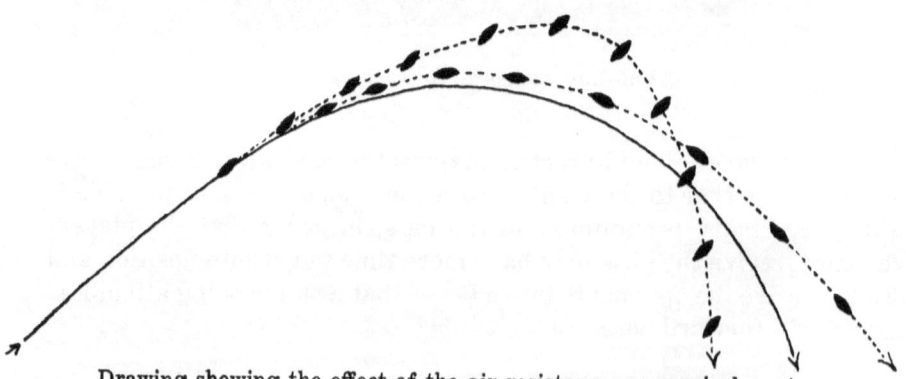

Drawing showing the effect of the air resistance upon spiral punts.

The two kinds of spirals described, travel through the first half of their course practically alike, and it is only in the last half, or after the ball begins to descend, when the difference in their position with reference to their course becomes apparent, and causes the air resistance to effect them differently. As explained above, the ball which keeps its front end pointed in the direction of its flight will carry farther, because of less resistance to the air, but this is not the only reason. The ball in descending will tend to fall in the direction toward which its lower end points, since that is the direction or line of least resistance, and consequently, as shown in the diagram, the ball which maintains its same position with reference to the ground throughout its course will, in descending, not only meet more air resistance but will tend to slide down on the air in the direction pointed to by its rear end, and will fall several yards short of where a round ball, following a normal course, (represented in the diagram by the solid line) would fall.

On the other hand, the ball which keeps its end or long axis pointed in the direction it is tsaveling, presents its smallest possible surface to the air throughout its course, and consequently the air resistance is less, and it will travel faster and farther than will a round ball following a normal course.

The catcher should therefore watch the ball in its course and be governed, in getting under it, by the direction toward which its lower end is pointing while descending. When the spiral descends with its forward end nearest the ground, the catcher will understand that the ball will carry much farther than it will when it descends with its rear end inclined downward.

When the punt is judged correctly the catching of it is simply and easily accomplished, providing the player practices faithfully, and has obtained a correct knowledge of how it is done, either by being properly coached, or by studying out the best method himself.

I have observed a great many coaches teaching their backs to catch punts by forming a sort of pocket with their arms, body, and the thigh of one leg, into which the ball is supposed to fall and be held by the arms. I believe this method is not the best form, and that very few players catch punts that way, even when coached to do so. My observation and experience have convinced me that the best, simplest, and surest method of catching punts, is to simply pin the ball to the body with the hands the instant it lands there. The hands should be extended toward the ball as it is descending, so as to come down to the body with the ball, and no attempt should be made to catch the ball with the hands alone, except in cases where the ball has to be caught very close to the ground, or above the head.

These are snapshots of a famous player catching punts. The first picture shows him about to catch a high one, the second a low one, and the third shows how he pins the ball to his body with his hands. Many players can get better results by pinning the ball to the breast with one hand under it and the other on top.

An important fact to remember in catching punts, is that the eyes should not leave the ball an instant until it is caught. Many punts are fumbled because players take their eyes off the ball an instant to see where the opposing ends are and in what direction to run, and this habit usually proves disastrous. While watching the ball descend, the catcher can usually see out of the corner of his eyes where his opponents ends are and in what direction he had better start, and whether he can or not, the catching of the ball is the all-important matter to attend to first, the running of it back being an after consideration.

The punt having been caught, unless it is a fair catch, the ball should be quickly placed under the arm, and the player should start quickly and at top speed toward the opponent's goal. No time should be wasted in looking for an opening or in dodging back and forth across the field. Usually the best plan is to shoot straight ahead. Dodging back and forth looks pretty, and eluding several tacklers may create a little enthusiasm among the spectators who know little about the game, but the opposing forces are gathering all the time, and such **tactics** usually result in no gain or a loss, and the player is not raised any in the estimation of the coach, or those who understand or appreciate good football.

CATCHING FORWARD PASSES.

The handling of forward passes is much the same as catching punts, with the exception that the ball usually has to be taken while on the run, and while running with the back or side to the ball. The ends do a great deal of this work, and therefore they, as well as the backs, should practice catching passes while running in this way. Since these passes are usually caught while running with the ball, it is of course harder to catch them against the body, and the players should become accustomed to catching with the hands and in fact in all positions. In case the player cannot catch the ball he should, if possible, make an attempt to at least touch it, because by so doing he gives all other players of his own side besides himself the right to secure the ball before it touches the ground.

Showing correct positions and distances preliminary to a quick place-kick from scrimmage formation.

Place Kicking

The place kick is used in several different ways,—for goal kicking after touchdowns and after fair catches, for kicking goals from the field from scrimmage formation, and in kicking off.

The quick place kick from scrimmage formation is easier to develop than the drop kick, can be gotten off quicker, and in my opinion is more accurate and better suited to kicking field goals.

The player who is to receive the ball from the center should kneel upon his left knee (assuming that he is right handed and that the kicker is right footed) about seven or eight yards from the line of scrimmage, and facing to the left. He should mark the spot on the ground where he intends to place the ball, to enable the kicker to get his position and aim, and then extend his arms toward the center as a signal that he is ready. Upon receiving the ball he should quickly place it upon the spot he has marked, withdrawing his left hand and holding the ball in a perpendicular position with the forefinger of his right, which should be lifted from the ball an instant before the kicker's foot comes in contact with it.

Receiving and placing the ball is an important part in successful place kicking from scrimmage, and should be practiced fully as much as the place kick itself.

The kicker should stand about two yards back of the player who is to place the ball, with his feet together and the toe of his right foot on a line with the center of the goal and the spot where the ball is to be placed. The instant the ball touches the ground he should take a short step with his right foot, a longer one with his left, and as the latter is placed on the ground to the left of the ball and about eight inches back of it, the right leg should be swung straight from the hip

Showing the ball placed, and the player in the act of kicking a quick place-kick. Note that the player who has placed the ball, has raised his finger from it an instant before the kick is made. He has held the ball in position with his left hand. Most players can do it better with the right.

with the toe of the foot extended and meeting the ball near the ground so as to raise it above the scrimmage line. The kicker should keep his eyes upon the ball until after it is kickd. The force he puts into the kick should depend entirely upon the distance the ball has to travel in order to go over the cross-bar, and if near the goal, greater accuracy can be secured by kicking just hard enough to get the ball over it.

Goal Kicking After Touchdown.

The kicking of goals, after touchdowns have been made, is a much more important department of the game than is generally considered. Many games are won or lost by the kicking or the missing of a goal and every team should have at least two players who, by continued practice, have become expert in that line. In addition to being accurate, a good goal kicker should be a cool headed player who will not become nervous or rattled when much depends upon his success or failure to kick the goal, nor be bothered by the jibes of the opposing players. It is quite common, and an advantage, to have one of the five center men on the team do the goal kicking because, being usually large fellows, they do not as a rule have such high nervous temperaments as the backs and ends and as they have less running to do, they are not usually so much exhausted by the strenuous efforts put forth in securing the touchdown.

In determining the distance which the ball should be placed from the goal line, the first thing to consider is that the ball should be far enough away from the goal so that there will be no difficulty in raising it over the cross-bar, and this should be the determining factor in selecting the spot from which to kick the goal, provided the touchdown was made within ten or twelve yards from the center of the goal. As a matter of fact this includes nearly all trials for goal, because if the touchdown is made farther out to the side the ball should be, and usually is, punted out to a position more nearly in front of the goal.

Supposing the touchdown has been made directly between the goal posts, the ball should be carried out at least ten yards, because any shorter distance would make it too difficult to lift the ball over the bar. If the kicker has no difficulty in raising the ball over the bar from the ten yard line, he should not have it placed farther back, since it is obvious that the farther back the ball is placed the greater accuracy in direction will be required in driving it between the posts, as the angle formed by straight lines from the ball to the posts, becomes smaller as the distance from the goal increases. A great many goal kickers have trouble in lifting the ball over the bar from the ten yard line, and when this is the case the ball should be placed at some point between the ten and fifteen yard lines. It should never be carried out beyond the fifteen yard line unless the trial is to be made at a point within ten yards of the side line, where the twenty yard line will give the most favorable angle.

Having determined the spot from which the ball is to be kicked, the player who is to hold the ball, assuming the player is right footed, should lie on the ground on his left side with his body parallel to, and facing the goal line. He should rest the knuckle of his left hand upon the ground, letting the lower end of the ball rest upon his thumb and first finger so that it will be about three-quarters of an inch from the ground. Many players make the mistake of resting the ball on the first finger alone, but this is bad form for the reason that in withdrawing it after the ball is placed, there is danger of pulling the ball out of position. The first finger of the right hand should hold the ball on top, using the thumb and second finger to revolve the ball as directed by the kicker in order to get the seam directly in the center. The lace should be toward the goal. The kicker should direct the holder of the ball, using the words "top in," "top out," "seam in," or

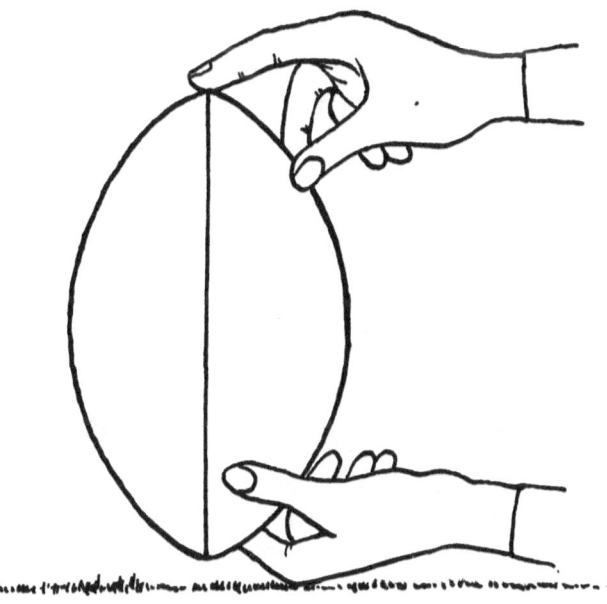

This drawing shows the correct method of holding the ball for goal kicking. When the kicker says "down" the ball is lowered to the ground and the thumb and fingers of the lower hand are withdrawn.

"seam out" until the ball is in a position exactly suited to him. The kicker should then get into position himself, standing back of the ball just far enough so that one step with his right foot will bring him to the proper kicking distance from the ball. He should stand with both feet together and with the toe of his right foot on a line with the ball and the center of the goal, unless there is a side wind in which case he should always make allowance for that in getting his aim. When in proper position himself, he should look again to see that the ball is still held true and having satisfied himself as to that, he should say "down," step forward with the left foot and kick the ball as explained previously, being sure to extend the toe downward, and meet the ball very close to the ground in order to raise it high enough to clear the bar, and looking always at the ball and not at the goal. There should be an understanding between the kicker and the man holding the ball that one definite word "down" will be used by the kicker to notify the holder when to place the ball, in order to avoid the danger of placing the ball at the wrong time through a misunderstanding. When the holder is instructed to place the ball he should lower it to the ground, release his thumb and finger from the lower end, and raise his finger from the top the instant before the toe of the kicker comes in contact with it.

The kicker should not kick any harder than is necessary to get the ball over the bar.

The ball should be in a perpendicular position when placed, although some kickers prefer to have it leaning slightly toward the goal, and others think they can get better results by having it lean slightly toward them.

The form of holding the ball and kicking it in trials for goal from fair catches, is the same as explained above, with the exception that the kicker may need to stand farther back, and take two steps in order to get force enough into the kick to carry it over the bar.

Kick Off

In kicking off, the ball should be teed up an inch or two, to enable the kicker to get under it and raise it well, and by experimenting the kicker will find that if he tees the ball up rather high with the aid of a little pile of dirt, and leans it at the proper angle toward the goal line, he will be able to drive his toe directly into the lower point of the ball and secure great height and better distance. Kicking the ball high is a very important thing in the kickoff, as a high kicked ball hangs in the air longer and enables the players of the kickers side to get farther down the field before the opponents can secure the ball and start back with it. Usually the kicker stands several yards back of the ball and takes a short run, in order to get as much force as possible into the kick.

When kicking off the kicker should be accurate enough to kick to either side and not directly down the center of the field, placing his kick upon the side of the field where the wind (if there is any) will aid the opponents the least or handicap them the most, notifying his teammates, of course, which side he intends to kick the ball. If the ball goes out of bounds upon the first trial, no chances should be taken on the second kick, but try to kick the ball straight down the field.

Drop Kicking.

TO become an expert drop kicker requires a great deal of perseverance and practice. Hudson, who played quarter back on the Carlisle teams of the late nineties, was probably the best drop kicker ever on the gridiron. He could drop kick with either foot and he obtained his skill by continued and faithful practice. During the winter he

About to drop the ball for a drop-kick. Instead of taking one step with the left foot, the player has stepped forward first with the right, or kicking foot, making it necessary to take two steps preliminary to the kick, which is advisable when considerable distance is required. For distances of twenty yards or less, greater accuracy can be secured by taking a single step with the left foot.

practiced in the gymnasium, using the parallel bars for a goal. Carlisle has nearly every year had a good drop kicker on her team, and the Indians have all followed the form or style used so successfully by Hudson, which is as follows:—The ball is held waist high and well away from the body directly in front of the right, or kicking foot, with its long axis perpendicular to the ground and the left hand, on the upper end of the ball, a bit to the left, and the right on its lower

The toe just meeting the ball as it rises from the ground. In the endeavor to meet the ball upon its lower end, the cleats of the player's shoe have scraped the ground as shown by the dust.

end, a bit to the right. The feet should be close together and the lace of the ball toward the goal. A step is taken forward with the left foot, the ball is dropped by simply taking the hands away from it so that it will strike the ground in a perpendicular position, and the right foot should meet it squarely just as the ball touches or is rising from the ground. The player should do his sighting before he starts the kick, and after he has the ball in his hands he should not take his eyes from it an instant until after the kick is made. The leg of the kicking foot should swing almost entirely from the hip and the toe should meet the ball very close to the ground.

The kicker should pay no attention whatever to the opponents who are breaking through to block the kick. If he follows this advice he will find he can drop kick as well in a big game as he can in practice. This tests a player's nerve, and one who drop kicks well in practice and makes repeated failures in the games is of little value to a team.

Many good drop kickers hold the ball with one hand on each side instead of with one hand under and one over it, and this is not bad form. The ball can be dropped accurately either way.

How to Play End.

AN end should be one of the headiest, quickest, and fastest men upon the team. He should be what is commonly called "foxy," and not easily fooled. He need not necessarily be as large as the guards, center, and tackles although the heavier an end is, provided he has the necessary speed and other qualifications, the more value he will be to his team. The tendency for several years has been to develop heavy ends. The game as now played requires speed and more skill in handling the ball, because of the open game and the handling of forward passes which devolves upon him, and these are qualities usually more highly developed in the smaller players, or those of medium weight, but the tackles and guards of the defending team now usually play so wide that their opposing tackles have to block the guards, and the end has to handle the tackle unaided. As the tackle is usually a strong and heavy man, the end whose duty it is to keep him from spoiling plays in his direction should be heavy enough to hold his own with him, or his team will be severely handicapped when upon the offense. Where heavy experienced material is scarce ,the lighter men are usually placed on the ends or back of the line, since weight is not so essential for those positions as for the five center men.

The end should be a low, sure tackler, able to avoid interference and tackle in the open, and he should be quick and sure in falling upon fumbled balls. He should also be able to handle forward passes without fumbling.

When his side has the ball, the end should stand as close to the line of scrimmage as possible, with the outside foot forward, and his inside hand or both hands upon the line, his back straight and parallel to the ground, and with his feet well apart to give him stability to withstand a charge or push from the side. He should face directly toward the opponent's goal ilne or at right angles to the line of scrimmage, and he should be about an arm's length from his tackle, and not allow the opposing tackle, by varying his position, to induce him to follow him. A foxy tackle will very likely move out wide or close in, in order to see if he can determine, by the action of the end, where the play is coming. If the end follows him out, so as to be in a position to box him in on an end play, it will give the play away; therefore the end should line up in one position with his eyes upon the ball, and he should maintain that position until the ball is snapped. If the tackle plays too wide for the end to be able to box him in, the remedy is for the quarter, or whoever is directing the plays ,to send plays inside of him. A few gains there will usually cause the tackle to close in, in order to defend his position.

The end should get into all regular plays which his quarter directs to the opposite side of the line outside of tackle, leaving his position with the snap of the ball, and following up the play to make the play safe. As he is the last man in the play, his particular duty is to watch out for fumbles, and quickly fall upon the ball or tackle the opponent who may secure it. On plays which are aimed on the opposite side of the line inside of tackle the end should go through and block off one of the secondary defense, since under the new rules he is prevented from going behind to push. On plays which are aimed at his side of the line, the end should block the tackle. If the play is between center and guard, he should shoulder his opposing tackle out and go through and block off one of the backs, or interfere for the runner if the latter succeeds in getting through the line. Should the play be between the opposing guard and tackle, or directed at the tackle, he should charge his man back and outward, and stay with him until the play is stopped or the runner has passed. The end must block the tackle in when the play is outside of his position or, should the tackle be playing outside of him he may drive him back; but he must neither let him break through, nor allow his opponent to push him back into the play. The tackle is a very dangerous man on plays of this kind, and unless he is pushed out of the way or blocked, the play will usually fail. As explained in the discussion of blocking and interfering, the end can make good use of his legs in preventing the tackle from getting to the runner, and he should not depend upon his shoulder alone.

On short forward passes, where he is supposed to be in a certain position to secure the ball, the end should try to deceive his opponents by first blocking his man a moment, and then run quickly to the spot where he is supposed to secure the pass. On long passes he should leave his position upon the snap of the ball and get to the spot as quickly as he can. He must be able to catch the ball while running with his side or back to it ,and should practice this until he is able to catch passes in any position.

On regular punts from scrimmage, kick-offs, trials for goals from fair catches, and punt-outs following touchbacks and safeties, the end should move out from his tackle from five to ten yards, and go down the field the instant the ball is put in play. He should not look back over his shoulder until he hears the thud of the kicker's foot as it meets the ball. He should keep well to the outside of the spot where the ball is going, as he is the outside man and if the player who secures the ball gets around him, he will make a good gain before the other tacklers can get to him, whereas, even if the end is not able to tackle the man himself, if he forces him to go inside of him he will drive him toward others of his side, who will very likely down the runner before he has been able to make much progress. The end should be careful when nearing the man who has secured or is about to catch the ball, and slow up so that he may not over-run him, nor allow the man to side-step or dodge him.

On defense the end should play about three to five yards from the tackle, the proper distance varying according to the system of defense his team is using. His duties will also vary on different teams for the same reason, and, therefore, I will only outline the duties that usually devolve upon the end under all systems of defense.

At the proper distance from the tackle, the end should assume a position similar to a sprinter on his mark, so as to be able to get a quick start. He should face slightly towards the backs of the opposing team, watch the ball, and as soon as it is moved, start almost straight forward, and not directly towards the backs. After he has his start, he can then see where the play is aimed, and vary his course accordingly. If the play is coming toward his position, he should meet it quickly and not hesitate or wait for the interference to get to him. He should keep well to the outside of the play, so that he will force the play inside of him and toward his mates, if he is not able to tackle the runner or stop the play himself. He should keep very close to the ground, and if he can avoid or work his way through the interference and secure the runner, he should do so. If the interference is close and the runner well protected, he should hurl his body across the knees of the interferers, and the chances are that as they fall, the runner will fall over them or will be forced to slow up to get around the pile and, unprotected, he becomes an easy prey for the tackle or backs. The main things for an end to remember are, first—that he must never wait for the play to come to him, and second—that he must meet it with his body close to the ground, and not standing up, where the interferers can get at him with their shoulders.

If the play is aimed at or just inside the tackle on his side, the end will be able to see it as he charges forward, and can throw himself inward and often tackle the runner from the side; but he should watch out, and not do this unless he sees the ball in the player's arms, as the play may be a fake to draw him in.

If the play is aimed at the center, or at the other side of the line, the end should follow it up as fast as he can, being careful not to over-run any delayed passes or criss-cross plays. An excellent plan to adopt in following up plays from behind, is to make it a point to always run over the place where the backs stood when starting, and then if there is anyone of them waiting to receive a delayed pass, the end will run over him. Having caught up with the play, the end should tackle the runner from behind if possible, and at all times he should be on the watch for fumbles. Under no circumstances should an end ever run around behind his own line to head off a play.

When the other side forms for a punt, the end should, as a rule, play about five to seven yards back of the line and about the same distance out beyond his tackle, no matter whether the opposing end moves out or not. He will then be in a position where he can follow the opposing end down the field in case the ball is punted or a pass is made, or rush up to head off the runner if it is a fake kick. He should not leave his position until he is sure what the play is to be. When he sees the ball punted, he should follow down the field on the inside of his opponent, bothering him all he can, and as the opponent slows up preparatory to tackling, the end should hurl his body at his knees or, if behind, drop on his legs and pin him to the ground.

If the opponents attempt a forward pass from the punt formation the end, if playing back of the line of scrimmage, can usually size up the play before the pass is made and he should cover the half back on his side of center, leaving the defensive back on his side to cover the end.

Some coaches play their ends upon the line on the punt formation and in that case they rush in to hurry the pass, block the punt or tackle the runner in case an end run is attempted, leaving the defensive backs to block the opposing ends on punts or to intercept forward passes.

On all plays, the defending end should watch any opposing end or half-back who starts to run wide as the ball is snapped, for in such cases the play is likely to be a forward pass, and he should quickly follow the opponent out.

Whenever a ball goes out of bounds, the defending end on that side of the field should be the last man to leave the side-line when the ball is brought in, and he should see that no player is left on the side line to receive the ball on a trick play. He should also be careful, after every play, that no opponent is left outside of his position unnoticed for a similar purpose.

The end should watch the ball closely and follow it swiftly at all times.

How to Play Tackle.

THE position of tackle is one of the most important upon the team. Two good tackles are a valuable asset to any team, and in these positions the fastest and most experienced big men of the squad should be placed, since good, heavy, active tackles can do more damage to the opponent's offense than players in any other positions upon the line. Weight is not quite to essential for this position as for the position of guard, and speed is of less importance than for the position of end, but a player who possesses both weight and speed, combined with a thorough knowledge of the game, should make an ideal tackle.

OFFENSE

When his team has the ball, the tackle should stand as far forward as the rules allow, and about an arm's length from the guard. He should maintain this position no matter how wide his opponent plays. He should have his outside foot forward, his inside or both hands upon the line, and his legs should be well under him and far enough apart so as to give him stability to withstand a side push. He should face squarely to the line of scrimmage, with his head up, and his back straight and parallel to the ground. He should keep his eyes upon the ball. He should not, by the least look or movement, give his opponents an inkling as to where the play is to be directed, and in every play he should start the instant the ball is put in play or the starting signal is given.

On regular plays directed to the opposite side of the line outside of tackle, he should leave his position, to interfere on end runs. In starting for that purpose he should push off with the foot and hand which are upon the line, and his first step should carry him back far enough so that he will not stumble over the legs of the other linemen.

If the play is to go inside of tackle on the other side, he should block the tackle temporarily, and then go through to block off one of the defending backs, but if the play is directed between guard and center on his side, he should let the end take care of the tackle and he himself help the guard with his man. On plays outside of the guard, on his side of the line, whether end or tackle plays, the tackle should, as a rule, block the opposing guard, as this player usually plays so wide that his opponent is unable to box him in without help. The opposing tackle is usually beyond his blocking range on these plays, and will have to be taken care of by the end and the interference. Of course if the opposing guard and tackle are playing close in, the guard will then take care of his man alone, and the tackle will aid the end in putting the opposing tackle out of the play. The tackle will have to use his own judgment as to which of the opponents to block, being governed by their positions upon the line; but the end and guard should always know which one of them he is to aid on these plays.

When his team punts, the tackle need not block as long as the guards, and by a quick charge or a hard side push, he should be able to prevent his opponent from interfering with the punt, and at the same time get a quick start down the field to aid the ends in preventing the ball from being run back. The left tackle especially, provided the punter is right-footed, need hardly hesitate at all before going down the field, since his opponent, after being pushed outward, can very seldom ever get over in front of a right-footed punter.

DEFENSE

On the defense the tackle should play about a yard and a half from his guard, and close upon the line of scrimmage. He need not play quite so low as when upon the offense, but it is well to have at least the inside hand upon the ground. He may face slightly toward the opposing backs, and should shift his position from time to time, in order to try and induce the opposng end to make some move which will give him a hint as to the direction of the play. He should note the formation of the opponents in order that, should there be more strength upon one side of the ball than the other, he can shift his position accordingly. Having gotten his position and his bearings, he should then watch the ball in order to get a quick charge. The instant the ball is snapped, the tackle should charge straight at the opposing end, who will very likely be in front of him, meeting him on the shoulders with the arms extended, and driving him back if possible. He should at least prevent the end from getting his body or shoulder against him, or from forcing him back. After charging, the tackle will note the direction of the play. If it is directed outside of his position, he should push the end in and work his way out, in order to tackle the runner or break up the interference. If the play is aimed directly at his position or to the inside, he can either push the end back into it or to the outside, and fall in front of the play himself.

If the play is directed to the opposite side of the line, the tackle should follow it up to tackle from behind, always watching for fakes and fumbles. When the opponents form for a punt, the tackle should endeavor to break through the line and block the kick, unless he has been instructed in such cases to block his opponent from running down the field. The left tackle is in the better position to block the punts of a right-footed kicker, and as a rule he should always go through to block or hurry the kick, while the right tackle can usually render better service by blocking his opponent.

At all times, whether upon the defense or offense, the tackle should follow the ball closely, and as he is usually a big, aggressive player, he should make it a point to protect the backs of his team and assist them to their feet whenever possible.

The one great thing for the tackle to remember, especially when on the defense, is that he should be a veritable tiger, fighting his way to the man with the ball, and fiercely overcoming all opposition with a determination that cannot be denied.

How to Play the Position of Guard.

QUALIFICATIONS

THE position of guard on a football team requires the least experience of any position on the team, for the reason that a guard has less territory to cover, and his duties are better defined than those of any other player. He has less opportunity for tackling, seldom runs with the ball and can play a good game without being able to catch punts or kick. He has few chances to make sensational plays, and yet the backs on his team could gain little ground but for his aid and protection.

The guard should be one of the heaviest men on the team, because strength to withstand the attacks and break up the opponent's plays when they have the ball, and to make openings and protect the backs when his own team is on the offense—is the main qualification necessary to play his position.

While it is not necessary for the guard to be a particularly fast runner, he should by all means develop quickness in starting, and a good leg drive, as these are absolutely essential to fast and effective charging. A quick start and fair speed are required in getting into the interference on plays around the opposite end, and no guard should be given a place upon the team unless he is active and fast enough for this. Under the new rules weight will not be so essential as speed, because of the partial elimination of mass plays.

POSITION

A guard should stand with his feet on the diagonally opposite corners of a square (or of a rectangle, if he is particularly long legged) with both feet and his whole body pointing straight ahead or at right angles with the line of scrimmage. The left guard should have his left foot forward and vice-versa, in order to enable him to more readily get into the interference on plays going around the opposite side. He should have the fingers of his inside or both hands touching the ground, his head up, and his back straight and no part of it higher than his shoulders, so that when he charges against his opponent his body has an upward drive. The lower he can stand the better, for when two men charge each other, the one who keeps the lower and has an upward drive, has a great advantage. He should keep his head up, so that he can watch the ball and the opposing backs, as well as his immediate opponents.

DEFENSE

The most successful and most generally adopted position for a guard, in playing on the defensive, is as above described, with *both* hands upon the ground, and at a distance of a good arm's length from his center. If the formation of the opponents is regular, the guard's position should be a little outside of his opponent, but he should shift to the right or left, as the case may be, if he sees the opponents have a one-sided formation.

A guard's duties on defense, are chiefly to protect his position, and the space between him and his tackle, from plays aimed at those places, and he may be able, by pushing his opponent into them, to aid in stopping plays aimed at the center.

When the opponents have the ball, the guard should note the formation of the opposing backs, and then keep his eyes upon the ball. He will be able to see the position of his opponent while watching the ball, and if the opponents are slow in forming, he can oftentimes determine, by looking at the backs, upon which side of the line the play will come, because very often some back will give the play away by his actions. A guard should *always charge the instant the ball is snapped*. This rule is invariable, whether on offense or defense; for the man who "gets the charge" on his opponent has a great advantage. If the guard sees the play coming at him, he may either throw his opponent to one side, and himself drop in front of the play at the knees of the oncoming men, or charge his opponent back directly in front of the play. If the play is not coming into his territory, he should charge through (not allowing his opponent to block him) and if he cannot get the man with the ball, he will be able, with shoulders and body, to cut off several players who are interfering. While playing this way he must *watch the ball*, and make sure that no criss-cross or "split play" comes through his position. If the play goes around the opposite side, he should follow around at top speed, and by so doing he can often catch the runner from behind, or keep him from making a successful forward pass.

The guard should follow the ball *always*. By charging through fast, with his eyes always on the ball, he can prevent the opposite backs from getting off quick kicks and forward passes. When the opposing team kicks, he must charge through fast, and attempt to block the kick by jumping in the air and throwing up his arms at the proper time. He must also be keen to see and frustrate a fake kick through the line.

OFFENSE

On the offense the guard should play close to the center and it is not necessary that he should have both hands upon the ground, although this is the position most generally assumed. If only one hand is upon the ground it should be the hand nearest the center and the opposite elbow should rest upon the knee.

A guard must never allow his oponent to charge through and interfere with the plays or the quarter passing the ball, and he should never allow his opponent to charge him back. He should, is possible, always "get the charge" on his opponent. In making holes for plays, the guard need not, and often cannot, get his opponent entirely out of the path of the play, but he should get his own body on the same side of his opponent that the play is coming, and charge him backward and away from the play. If he is unable to move his opponent, but gets under him and gets the charge on him, the backs, with their momentum when they hit the line, will force the opponent backward, and the play will gain ground. A guard can often, by being "foxy," mislead his opponent as to where the play will come, so that the opponent will almost get himself out of the way by charging in the wrong direction. A guard should "size up" his opponent so that he can take advantage of his weakness and more easily get him out of the way. If he stands high, the guard may charge under him and up, so that when the backs strike the line he will go over backwards. If he stands so low that it is impossible to get under him, his head can be pushed to the ground so that he cannot see or get at the play.

One of the chief points of a guard's usefulness to his team, is in leading or getting into the interference on plays going around the opposite end. He should start the instant the ball is snapped by stepping with the rear foot backwards, so that he will be clear of the center, shoving off with the forward foot, and then bringing it around so that he is in full stride. He may also help to start himself by quickly slapping or pushing the center forward with his nearer hand as he steps backward, thereby helping himself to turn, and giving the center a forward impetus at the same time. He should run with knees high and ward off tacklers with shoulders and body.

A guard should always be standing over the back who has been tackled, ready to help him up and give him an encouraging word. The backs are usually smaller men, they get some severe jolts from the opposing tacklers, and the aid and protection of the big line-men help them materially.

A guard should always, on offensive or defensive, "line-up" or get into position as soon as the ball is in place. After a play, particularly a line play, has passed the line and the guard has charged his opponent out of the way, he should continue with the runner, blocking off the secondary defense and warding off tacklers.

When a punt is planned, a guard's first duty is to prevent any one coming through his territory and blocking the kick. He need not block longer than to allow the punter to get the kick off safely, then he should get down the field at top speed and tackle the man who catches the punt, or be ready to get the ball if it is fumbled. If the guard finds that no back attempts to block the punt by coming through his territory, he can often, by making an extra-quick start and hard charge, get his opponent off his feet, or tangled up at one side, and himself get away down the field almost as quickly as the ends; and when he once gets started he usually has a clear field, for very seldom are men coached to block him as they do the ends. Getting down the field on kicks in this way will give the guard more chance to make open-field tackles than he is liable to get at any other time during the game, except upon kick-offs, where he has the same opportunity.

The guard, besides having strength, must have confidence in himself and never, at any stage of the game or under any circumstances, show signs of weakening. His opponent will very likely play his hardest and roughest and do considerable bluffing early in the game, in order to test the guard's nerve, strength, and mettle, and if he succeeds in bulldozing or getting the better of him, it will give the opponent encouragement and confidence which wll cause him to play harder as the game progresses, whereas a good stiff opposition will tend to have the opposite effect.

How to Play Center.

THE center should be a heavy man, and at the same time an active player with a good head, steady, and not easily rattled. Many good centers have been comparatively small players, but weight combined with activity, enables a player in this position to do better work, both upon the offense and when the opposing team has the ball.

Not so much experience is required for center as for ends, backs, and tackles, since a player in this position has less tackling to do, and his duties are not so varied as for the other positions mentioned. The center does not necessarily have to be a fast runner, since he has less running to do than any other player upan the team, but he should be active, nevertheless, and a quick charger.

The center is in a very conspicuous position, because he handles the ball in every play when his team is in possession of it, and the ball and the player in whose possesion it is, is always the center of interest and watched closely by the spectators.

On the offense the center should have his feet planted upon the diagonally opposite corners of a square of about two feet six inches each way. He should face directly at right angles to the line of scrimmage, with his knees well apart, so that he can move his arms between them freely in passing the ball back, and no part of his back should be higher than his shoulders. He should hold the ball with a hand upon each side of it and a little back of the center ,and with his elbows just inside his knees. The rear end of the ball should be about on a line with the toe of his forward foot.

He should note the position of his opponent ,and then watch the quarter, in order to be sure never to pass the ball when the quarter is not in position to receive it. If a starting signal is used, the ball is passed upon that, but if not, the center should pass the ball any time after the quarter is ready for it, being careful not to always pass the instant the quarter is ready, as this will cause the opposing line-men to watch the quarter and anticipate the snap of the ball, and therefore get the charge upon their opponents. **When passing the ball the center** should not look at the quarter, but at his opponent; and his charge and pass should be simultaneous—his arms moving backward with the ball and his body moving forward to block his opponent. With practice he will be able to pass well in this way, and pass accurately without looking at the quarter-back. Since the first man to receive the ball is now allowed to run anywhere with it, there will be a tendency to use plays in which the ball does not pass through the quarter-back's hands, but direct to the runner, and therefore good passing will be one of the most valuable assets of a center. On such passes he should look where he is passing.

In charging he should try to get his head on the side of his opponent on which the play is going and charge him back and away from the play with his shoulder and body. If the play is aimed outside of tackle he should go through after momentarily blocking his opponent, and block off one of the backs.

A very important thing for the center to remember is that he should always follow the ball closely, and be ready to take it from the runner as soon as the latter is stopped. This is necessary, because the runner should not leave the ball upon the ground unprotected, and the center should be there to receive it, in order to enable the man who has carried it to get back quickly into his position. A team cannot play a fast game if the center is slow in following the ball and getting into position for the next play. The opposing center may slyly push the ball back a few inches after each down unless he is watched closely and the ball is well protected, and this may prove costly to the offensive team in cases where the ball is lost on downs by a narrow margin.

In passing the ball back for a punt, the center should practice the long pass until he can get the ball back swiftly and accurately without first moving or raising the ball from the ground, and on these passes he should watch the man to whom the pass is made, and take a great deal of care in getting the ball to him cleanly. If the punter has to reach high or low or to the side to get the ball, it throws him out of position and interferes with his punting. It also makes the liability of a fumble greater. Great care should be taken not to pass the ball too high, because it may go over the punter's head with disastrous results. The pass had better be too low than too high. After passing the ball to the punter, the center should block his man long enough to prevent him getting through in time to block the kick, and then go down the field as fast as possible.

The method of playing center upon the defense differs according to the system of defense the team is using. Some centers are coached to play rather high, and back from the scrimmage line about a yard. In this position they watch the direction of the play and head it off wherever it is aimed, running around behind their own line if the play starts around the end or outside of tackle. By playing in this way the center can get into every play, and make the defense stronger in stopping plays in every direction except toward the center of the line. In order to play this method of defense properly, the center has to watch the backs and start the instant they start. If he sees the play start for his position, he goes into it and meets it low. The weak point in playing defensive center in this manner, is that it renders the center of the line more vulnerable to regular line-bucking plays, and especially to fake plays which start for some other point to draw the center away and then shoot through the unguarded positon

If the center plays in the line upon the defense he should play low, with both hands upon the ground, watching the ball and charging through the line, either to the right or left of his opponent, and vary- in this by occasionally charging his opponent back upon the quarter. By playing in this way the player gets a quicker charge, because he is in a better charging position, is watching the ball instead of the backs, and never hesitates to see where the play is going before the charge is made. He is also better able to guard the center of the line from fake as well as regular line plays, because the player is always going through and will meet it.

The center should usually move over, if the opponents have more strength upon one side of the ball than upon the other, and go through upon that side. In always going through, or charging his man back, the center will not only meet any play coming at him, but should the play be going around either end he will block off the line interference, and by following up the play, can very often tackle the runner from behind. If he happens to charge through one side, and the play comes through upon the other side of center, there will of course be an opening there; but a good defensive back is usually back- ing up the center, and the opening in the line will enable the defensive back to meet the play before it reaches the hole, or at least before the line is crossed.

The center should always get to the ball quickly when on the defense, as well as when his own side has the ball, not only because any good defensive player always follows the ball closely, but because, if he is not on the spot when the opposing center takes the ball from the runner, the latter will often move it ahead, in placing it in position for the next scrimmage, and thus gain a few inches on every play. The defensive center should not only prevent this, but should also watch his opponent when bringing in the ball from out of bounds, and see that he does not gain any ground by the operation, but brings it in at right angles to the spot where it went out.

When the other side forms for a kick, the center should play high, and either go through to block the kick and hurry the kicker, or, by prearrangement, make a hole for some other player to go through.

How to Play Quarter-back.

THE quarter-back position is without question the most important upon the team. The quarter is to his team what a general is to an army and needs to possess the same qualities of leadership—fearlessness, confidence in himself and in his men, enthusiasm, ginger, and above all a good head. The quarter should also be very clever in handling the ball, because in many plays the ball must go through his hands and be passed on tothe runner in such a manner that the latter has no trouble whatever in getting it. In addition to these qualities, the quarter should be an expert in handling punts and a sure tackler, because he is usually stationed in the full-back's position in the backfield when the opponents have the ball.

The quarter is usually a small or medium-sized player, since players of this type more usually possess the qualities necessary to play the position. A great many excellent quarter-backs, however, have been large men, and provided he possesses the necessary speed and skill, a heavy player will be able to accomplish more than a man of lighter weight. One reason why so many quarters have been of small stature, is because the larger men try for other positions, and by custom the little fellows upon the squad seem to be conceded the position of quarterback.

Since the rules now permit the first man to receive the ball from the center to run anywhere with it, the tendency will be to use direct passes from the center to the runner and therefore the quarter-back will not need to handle the ball so much as formerly. Under these conditions the quarter-back should possess the same qualities as half-backs and full-backs, since he will do much running with the ball and interfering.

The proper position for the quarter to assume, in receiving the ball from the center, is largely a matter of practice and choice. The quarter-backs of many prominent teams are coached differently in this respect, some of them playing close up, with their arms extended under the center, who simply hands them the ball; others standing with their back to one side line and facing the other; and still others standing back about a yard and a half or two yards from the center, and facing directly toward it. The main things to be considered in deciding upon the position which the quarter should assume, are that the ball must be handled cleanly, passed on to the runner in such a manner that the latter will not have to slow up or hesitate an instant in securing it, and the quarter must be in such a position after passing the ball that he can get into the interference.

The simplest, easiest to learn, and I believe the best position for a quarter to assume in receiving the ball from the snapper-back, is about a yard and a half to two yards back of the ball, directly facing it. His feet should be about two feet apart, his elbows or fore-arms should rest upon his thighs, and his hands should be extended toward the ball, wide open and with thumbs pointed outward. He should be just far enough back and low enough, to be able to see the ball. This position is assumed after he has looked over the formation of his opponents, decided what play to use, and given the signal, although he may be in position while giving the signal, and must be in case one of the numbers given is used as a starting signal.

The first snap-shot shows a pass for a line plunge, and the other for a play outside of tackle. Note that in the line plunge the quarter has placed the ball against the runner's stomach, and is holding it there while the latter is closing his hands and arms upon it.

If no starting signal is used, the center should pass the ball when he and the quarter are ready, and the latter should give no signal with his hands, as this will be watched by the opponents and used by them as a charging signal, thus giving them the advantage over the opposing line-men who are starting with the snap of the ball. The opposing team will watch closely the movements of the quarter, and if possible try to anticipate the snap of the ball by some movement he makes, and therefore the quarter should make no motion after getting into position, and the ball should not always be snapped as soon as the quarter is ready, as the opponents will thus soon be able to time the snap, and charge as soon as the quarter has his hands in position. This is important, and care should be taken that the opposing team can only time their charge by the actual snap of the ball.

The pass from the center should be received by the quarter against his stomach, the ball being pinned there by his hands.

The quarter should always pass the ball to the runner with one hand, using the left hand if the play is aimed at the quarter's right, and the right hand if the attack is to the left.

It is generally best for the quarter, in line plays, to advance at the runner's side and help bend back the line.

On plays outside of tackle, the quarter should get into the interference. This he can easily do by starting while he is receiving the snap-back, being sure to step first with the foot on the side toward which the run is to be made, and pushing off with the other. The pass should be made after the quarter is in motion, and care should be exercised in making it just the right height and in front of the runner, so that he will not have to slow up or reach back to get it. The pass should not be swift or hard, as this increases the chances of a fumble and nothing is to be gained by it. After passing the ball, the quarter should not watch to see whether the runner gets it or not, but should look ahead, and devote his entire attention to blocking the opponents who may get in the path of the runner.

It is very necessary that a quarter-back should possess the ability to pick out the right plays, and give the signals in such a way that they will be easily comprehended and at the same time put ginger and confidence into his team. It is a fact quite generally recognized, that the team will execute the plays in about the same spirit in which the quarter-back gives the signals for them. If he drawls the numbers out slowly and deliberately, the team will very likely play in about the same way, while if he calls out the signals in a snappy way, biting off the words sharply, his team will show more snap and ginger in executing his orders.

The quarter should never for a moment exhibit the least sign to the other players that he has lost confidence in his team's ability to gain ground. If the strongest plays do not gain at the beginning of the game, the quarter is likely to be at a loss as to what to do next, but it would be fatal to let his team see any signs of hesitancy or discouragement.

The quarter should be skilled in passing the ball, both for short and long distances, as he is the player who generally makes the forward passes. Many quarter-backs do the punting for their team, and it is an asset for any quarter to be able to punt, and place or drop-kick goals from the field.

The duties of quarter-back upon the offense have been explained thus far under the assumption that he will do the passing from center to runner, but as explained heretofore, many teams will use the direct pass from center to runner. The quarter-back position will then practically be done away with and he will simply be one of the backs who will run the ends, buck the line and interfere the same as the rest of the back field. In this case any one of the backs can give the signals and they can be changed about upon offense so as to give each man the department of play for which he is best suited.

On the defense, the quarter is usually stationed in the extreme back field, and in that position he has to handle punts and be a sure tackler. These departments of the game are treated thoroughly under separate heads and need not be dwelt upon here.

The quarter on defense (if he is playing in the extreme back field) should play about twenty-five or thirty yards back of the line of scrimmage, the distance depending upon whether or not the opposing team is favored in punting by the wind, and upon the punting ability of their kickers. The quarter should also take into consideration the liability of the opponents to punt or run with the ball under certain conditions and on certain downs, and play a little closer to the line when he is reasonably sure the play is to be a running one. Whenever a play starts (if it is a run) the quarter should run up as fast as he can to meet it, and often he will be able in this way, to prevent a long end run, and tackle the runner for no gain after the latter has circled the end and is turning down the field. A play through the line can be met by the quarter after everyone else has been passed, and stopped for a short gain, whereas if the quarter waits for such a play, the runner gains speed, has time to plan how to elude him, and therefore stands a better chance of getting clear, and even if tackled successfully, has already made a good gain which might have been cut down if the quarter had run up to meet the play.

The quarter, in his back field position, has all the players of both teams within his range of vision, and he should watch closely after each play of the opponents, and especially when the ball is brought in from out of bounds, and see that no player is left unnoticed out to the side for the purpose of executing a trick or receiving a long pass. If he sees anything of this nature, he should yell out to his team and call the attention of his ends to the situation.

As the opponents near his goal line, the quarter gradually lessens the distance he stands from the line, and when the ball is within the ten yard line, he should get into every play with all the force he possesses, depending upon the half-backs to guard against forward passes when near the goal line.

Under no circumstances should any player ever become discouraged or cease to put forth his best efforts, and the quarter-back should be the last man on his team to show any signs of weakening, always remembering that "the battle is not always to the strong, but to the active, the vigilant, and the brave."

How to Play Half-back and Full-back.

THE duties of the half-back and full-back, and the qualifications necessary for those positions, are so nearly alike that they will be treated under one heading.

In order to fill either of these positions satisfactorily, a player should be at least of medium weight, and the larger he is the better, provided he is active and a fast, strong runner, and can handle the ball cleverly. It is quite a general custom to place the heaviest back in the full-back position, since this player is used more than the others in bucking the line, and his weight is also useful in forming interference for the half-backs upon plays outside of tackle.

Whether he is to play full-back or half-back, the player should be of rugged build, so as to be able to stand hard knocks, because he runs with the ball more than most of the other players and the player who carries the ball is nearly always in the center of the scrimmage, and must stand the shock of being tackled and thrown to the ground many times during a game.

The half-back should not only be a fast, strong runner, but he must be clever in dodging opposing tacklers, skilled in warding them off by the use of the stiff-arm, and both half and full-back should be able to hold on to the ball, no matter how hard they are tackled or fall. They should be well drilled in all the rudiments of the game, especially in falling upon the ball, interfering, tackling, punting, and catching punts. They should be quick to think and act, and above all they should be fearless.

The half-back's position, when his team is in possession of the ball, will vary according to the formation used. Ordinarily he should be between four and five yards from the scrimmage line, and a good arm's length from the full-back, who stands behind the center. A player in either of these positions should stand with his feet about two feet apart, and with one, or better still, both hands upon the ground, with his head up, and no part of his body higher than his head and shoulders. His feet should be about even with each other, but if playing half-back the foot nearest the full-back may be a little back of his outside foot, bringing the player into the position of a sprinter upon his mark, except that his legs are farther apart. The player's weight should be about equally borne by his feet and hands. If the player places himself upon a two-foot square, his feet planted upon its rear corners and his hands resting upon the forward corners, with his shoulders almost directly over the latter, and his knees almost touching his elbows, he will find himself in the proper position, and be able to start quickly forward, or to the right or left. This position of the offensive backs was first introduced by the Indians when they defeated Columbia University 45-0, on Thanksgiving day, 1899, and has since been adopted by every team of prominence in the country.

When in position, the back should watch the ball, and start the instant it is snapped or the starting signal is given. If he is to take the ball outside of tackle, he should receive it upon the run, and quickly place it under the arm which is farthest away from the greatest number of the opponents, so that he can use the other arm to ward off tacklers. In placing the ball for such a play, one end of it should be held between the arm and body, and the hand should grasp the other end. (The pictures illustrating different methods of blocking and interfering show a player holding the ball correctly, and also the free arm in position to ward off tacklers.)

On plays through the line, the back should, as a rule, hold the ball against his body or under one arm with both hands, otherwise there is danger of his arm being jerked away from it, or the ball being pulled from his grasp, while forcing his way through the mass of players.

Now that the rules permit the first man receiving the ball to run with it without crossing the line five yards from center there will be much direct passing from center to backs and therefore the backs will need much practice in so receiving the ball on the run in order to avoid disastrous fumbles.

On end runs or plays outside of tackle, the back carrying the ball should follow his interference closely as long as it affords him protection, and not depend upon his individual efforts. He should turn toward the opponent's goal whenever he sees an opening, and not try to circle the end unless he is reasonably sure of being sucessful. A wide run of this kind usually results in no gain or a loss, whereas a quick turn straight down the field will usually gain something, or at least not result in a loss.

In trying to avoid tackles, the man carrying the ball should use his free arm to push would-be tacklers out of his path, meeting them on the head, shoulders, or neck, with the heel of the open hand, and with the arm held rigidly straight. At the same time he should swing his legs and body as far away from the tackler as possible. When tackled he should, if possible, fall toward the opponent's goal, and work his way forward until held or the whistle is blown.

Having explained the duties of a back when carrying the ball, an explanation of his duties when another player as carrying it is next in order. A back should remember that his part in nearly every play is just as important when someone else is carrying the ball as when he himself carries it, and he should put forth just as much effort to make the play successful. Some backs are inclined to run hard when they have the ball, and rest up or make a feeble effort when some one else is trying to advance it. Such tactics will soon be noticed by the rest of the team and by the spectators, and a player who puts forth his best efforts only when carrying the ball will soon become deservedly unpopular, especially with his teammates.

The backs should at all times follow the ball and get into position quickly after each play.

Methods of blocking and interfering, how to punt, fall on the ball, pass, tackle, catch punts, etc., are treated under those headings, and every back should be expert in those rudiments of the game.

On the defense, the position and duties of the backs vary under different systems. In one system of defense quite generally used, the half-backs are stationed about three yards back of the scrimmage line, and just outside of the tackles, while the full-back is supposed to play back of the center about ten to fifteen yards. Another system of defense used by many teams places the half-backs about two yards outside of the tackles and about five yards from the line, and the full-back is stationed about two or three yards back of center. In both systems the backs move to the right or left, in case the opponents have a one-sided formation. In the first system the half-backs are supposed to back up the line and guard against all running plays of the opponents, while the full-back looks out for forward passes, and gets into other plays when he sees the play is a running one. Under the other system, the full-back backs up the line and gets into all running plays, while the half-backs look out for side kicks and forward passes, and also help stop other plays, being in especially good positions to stop end runs or plays outside of tackle.

The defensive backs should all stand with their feet about two feet apart, and with their hands upon their knees, so as to be able to start quickly forward, or to either side. They should watch the opposing backs closely, and if they form upon one side of the ball they should at once notify the rest of their team, as the line men are watching the ball and may not notice the formation of the opposing backs. The defensive backs should shift with the offensive formation, so as to always be in the same relative position to the center of the offensive strength of the opponents, no matter where the ball may be.

The backs who are backing up the line should watch the heads of the opposing backs, because their heads will be the first part of their body to move and indicate the direction of the play. If the play is aimed at the line it should be met hard and low, and if there is a hole made for the runner, the defensive back should not wait for the play to come through, but dive into the opening and nail the runner, or the man in front of him, before he has reached the line. Every play should be quickly headed off, whether coming toward the back or going around the opposite end.

Good, heady backs should be able to guess pretty closely what the opponents are likely to do, judging from the number of the down, distance to be gained, and position of the ball upon the gridiron, and they should vary their defensive position accordingly, closing in when the opponents only need two or three yards to gain a first down, and will most likely attack the line, and spreading out upon first downs and when there are more than five yards to gain, as under those conditions the opponents are likely to run the ends, or use a trick play, forward pass, or a punt.

Hard-tackling defensive backs, who get into every play, are a most powerful factor in any team's defense, and upon the best teams the backs are chosen as much for their defensive ability as for their skill in running with the ball and interfering.

Football Practice

A PLAYING knowledge of the game of football, a formidable defense and splendid team work, can only be secured as the result of weeks and months of regular practice. It is important, then, that this practice should be intelligently conducted, and it is hoped that the following discussion of methods of teaching rudiments, and suggestions as to how and what to practice, will materially aid both coaches and players in obtaining the best results with as little waste of time and effort as possible.

After the first few days of the season the practice of falling upon the ball, charging, tackling, punting, and catching punts, etc., usually becomes monotonous, hard, and uninteresting work for the players; so much so that some players will come to practice late, in order to miss this daily grind and be fresh for the scrimmage practice which usually follows it.

The practice of these rudiments is absolutely necessary in order that the players may become proficient in all departments of the game, and therefore plans should be devised and followed, which will make the practice preliminary to the scrimmage as interesting as possible, and not simply cold-blooded routine work. For instance, in practicing falling upon the ball, the squad can be divided into groups of eight, ten, or twelve; one half of each group placed upon one five-yard line, and the other half facing them five yards away, with the ball midway between them. If there are ten players in each group, the players upon each line are numbered off from one to five and a coach, or some player who is unable to do rough work on account of an injury, can call out a number from one to five, and the two players having that number will dive for the ball. Then the other numbers are called, and the players, not knowing when their turn will come, must all be on the alert. This method creates competition, makes the players alert and quick to charge forward upon a signal, and gives them practice, not only in falling upon the ball, but in blocking off an opponent at the same time. These groups may be placed in a circle instead of on lines five yards apart, being so numbered that the two players having the same number will be upon opposite sides of the circle. Another method of making the practice of falling upon the ball interesting is to place the players all upon the same line, number them off from the center to the ends so that two players have the same number, and then the coach or some other person, standing in the center, rolls the ball, calls one of the numbers, and the two having that number try to block each other off and fall upon the ball. This gives them interesting and practical experience in recovering a rolling ball, and such practice will prove valuable in these days of forward passes and intricate plays, when the ball is liable to be fumbled quite often during a game.

The practice of charging can be varied each day, on one day using the charging sled, and creating competition by placing an equal number at each side of center and stimulating the players to see which side can push the other around. The next day the charging practice can be confined to placing the whole squad of linemen upon a line in a charging position, and let them see who can drive their bodies forward upon the ground the farthest. After doing this a half dozen or more times, the practice can be varied by having the players jump to their feet after thus charging out upon the ground, and run five or ten yards. On another day the linemen can get good practice by lining up against each other, and trying to charge each other back upon the snap of the ball.

In nearly everything a player does in a game of football, a good leg drive is necessary. In tackling he crouches low, and drives his body forward with a strong leg drive. When falling on the ball, he shoots his body forward upon the ball by the leg drive. When interfering, he gets in a good leg drive while in the act of blocking off a tackler. When upon the defense, the linemen use it in charging and breaking through; and when their team has the ball, they use it in opening holes and in blocking.

Since the leg drive is so important, it should be carefully developed, and nothing develops it better than the charging sled, charging forward upon the ground, or pushing each other around as above described.

The tackling practice should be varied by one day using the bag or dummy, and another day tackling each other. In the latter practice the squad can again be divided into groups, a player of each group standing upon a certain mark about two yards from the tackler, and after being tackled, letting the tackler stand for the next man in line,— thus preventing one man from bearing the hardship of being tackled by all the others. The man being tackled should face at right angles to the tackler, and when all have practiced tackling in that way, his position should be reversed, so as to give the players practice in tackling a player going by them on either side. Instead of standing, the player who is to be tackled can run in front of the line of tacklers and use his free arm to ward them off. This should be varied by having the runner come straight at the tackler, and in that case it is well to have another player hold him by the hand to break his fall when thrown backward upon the ground. In all this tackling practice there is no need of running hard, or tackling roughly, correct form being the important thing strived for.

A good way to practice open field tackling, and at the same time develop the backs in the use of the stiff arm and in carrying the ball in the open field, is to place a lineman upon every other five-yard line from one goal to the other, and start the backs with the ball, one at a time, from one goal line, and let them endeavor to reach the other goal without being tackled any oftener than they can prevent. The linemen should be instructed not to cross the line in front of them, although they can move across the field from side to side, in order to keep in front of the runner. While this is very valuable practice, it is hard and rough work, especially for the backs, and should not be practiced more than about one day of the week. It can be varied by having the backs and linemen change positions, as the backs need practice in open field tackling, and it will benefit the linemen to practice running with the ball.

When practicing catching punts, the backs should not only catch the ball, but they should place it quickly under the arm and start down the field; and whenever they fumble or miss the catch, they should fall upon the ball. They will regard this as a penalty, and will be more careful to catch the ball than they would if they did not have to fall upon it when fumbled.

The backs and ends should practice making and receiving the forward pass. They should form in a circle about ten yards apart, and practice correct form in passing or throwing, and catching the ball. This practice can end with the players running around the circle, and passing and catching while upon the run.

There should be practice at least twice a week in running down upon punts. The backs should be stationed to receive the punts, working in pairs, one catching and the other interfering for him. The linemen should be spread out upon a line about five yards back of the ball, so as to give them a clear vision of it, and to enable the punter to kick far enough to give the backs a chance to catch the ball before the tacklers are upon them. The line men should be numbered off so that not more than three or four will have the same number and go down at one time. In this practice, the punter should direct the tacklers by calling out "right," "left," or "short," as soon as he notes the direction and distance he has punted.

In practicing the rudiments, the squad is usually divided, the backs being in one group and the line men in the other. The backs may then be practicing passing or punting and catching, while the line men are charging; or one bunch can be using the tackling dummy while the other is falling upon the ball, thus keeping all the players systematically busy at something.

System in practice is a great help, and is necessary where only a short time can be devoted each day to practice. An hour and a half is long enough for any squad to practice, provided the players are all on hand at the same hour, and the practice is systematized so that no time is wasted. The backs can usually hustle on their suits and get sufficient practice in punting and catching punts while the rest of the squad is gathering, and when all are out upon the field, the players can be divided into groups as explained, some groups doing one thing and some another. It is usually quite a waste of time to have the whole squad at the tackling dummy at once, because the players will have to stand idle so long awaiting their turn.

The preliminary practice of rudiments is usually followed each day by a fast signal practice. When learning new plays, each player's duties in them should be explained, and the plays run through slowly at first, until every player knows just where to run and what to do. After this, it should be the aim to develop speed in the execution of the plays and in lining up after each play is made. A short, fast, snappy signal practice is much better than a long, tedious one, and the latter should not be indulged in before a hard scrimmage, because the energy and strength of the players will be so used up by it that they are more likely to injure themselves in the scrimmage practice.

When there are not enough players upon the squad for two teams to engage in a scrimmage practice, such practice can usually be had by filling the positions of the defensive team upon one side of the ball, and aiming all the plays at that side.

The scrimmage should not be of more than twenty minutes duration as a rule, unless no preliminary practice is indulged in, and no players should be allowed to participate in it who are suffering from injuries, or who are not in good physical condition. When a player is injured, another should be quickly put in his place, so that the practice may be continued without delays. The practice game should be made as near like a regular game as possible, in order that the players, and especially the quarter-backs, may have an opportunity to use their heads and practice generalship.

The following program for a week's practice gives a fair idea of about how the squad should be handled from one game to another, assuming that a fairly hard game is played upon the Saturday preceding, and the Saturday ending the week.

MONDAY

Punting, catching punts, goal kicking, place and drop kicking, while the squad is gathering,—fifteen minutes.

Falling upon the ball,—ten minutes.

Squad is divided, the backs practicing tackling, while the line men practice charging,—fifteen minutes.

Line men practice tackling, while the backs practice starting,—fifteen minutes.

Ends join the squad of backs and practice passing, while the other line men practice starting,—ten minutes.

Blackboard talk, pointing out the mistakes of Saturday's game, and explaining new plays which are to be developed during the week,—twenty minutes.

Running through new plays and practicing signals,—twenty minutes.

Scrimmage for the substitutes, and others who were not worked hard in the game on Saturday. The new plays are tried, and regular players not in the scrimmage coach their substitutes,—fifteen minutes.

TUESDAY

Punting, catching, goal kicking, place and drop kicking, while the squad is gathering,—twenty minutes.

Omit general falling upon the ball.

Backs practice tackling each other, while the line men practice breaking through and charging each other,—fifteen minutes.

Line men tackle each other, while the backs fall upon the ball—stationary and rolling—two going after it at once, as explained previously,—fifteen minutes.

Omit practice in passing.

Running down under punts,—twenty minutes.

Running through signals,—twenty minutes.

Scrimmage for all who are able to play,—ten minute halves with five minutes intermission.

WEDNESDAY

Same practice as upon Monday and Tuesday, while squad is gathering,—twenty minutes.

Open field running with the ball and tackling, as previously described,—fifteen minutes.

Backs and ends practice passing and catching, while the line men practice falling upon the ball in competition,—fifteen minutes.

Omit tackling, charging, and running down under punts, as the scrimmage should be made the main part of the practice on this day.

Running through signals,—fifteen minutes.

Scrimmage as near like a regular game as possible,- two twenty minute halves with ten minutes intermission.

THURSDAY

The same program as upon Monday, with the exception that all the uninjured get into the scrimmage.

FRIDAY

Punting, catching punts, goal kicking, and quick place, or drop kicking, the same as upon other days, but the kickers should ease up in their kicking and save themselves for the game on the following day.

Practice falling upon the ball, tackling and charging, but omit running down on punts.

Short, but fast, signal practice and the interference for running back kick-offs; also practice the punt out.

Omit the scrimmage and make the practice shorter than upon other days.

This program assumes that the squad has two hours for practice. If the practice period is shorter, the program can be shortened in places, and about the same amount of work done by hustling the players through it—keeping them upon the jump all the time, and allowing no loafing or fooling.

After a hard game, it will benefit the players greatly to take a walk of two or three miles into the country on Sunday afternoon.

Systems of Signals

THE signals should be simple and easily learned. Many of the smaller teams have been accustomed to numbering the players and the spaces between and outside of the players on the line, the first or second number given indicating the player who is to carry the ball, and the next number indicating the place to be attacked. This is not a good system of signals for several reasons, one of which is that it will generally prevent good team work, because the players, other than the one who is to carry the ball and the ones in the line where the attack is to be made, are likely to forget what they are to do, as the system compels them to figure out the play before the ball is snapped. Another reason why this system is not good is because it is not elastic enough and will not permit of enough combinations. There may be two or more plays where the same player carries the ball at a certain spot in the line, the plays differing in the manner in which they are played. Then again, under this system there is no good way to signal for fakes and forward passes, or any play where the ball passes through more than one man's hands besides the quarter-back.

It is a much better plan to have each play numbered, so that when a certain number is brought to the attention of the players it will instantly suggest the play—not simply which man is to carry the ball and where he is to run with it, but every player's part in the play. Nearly all the best teams have adopted this plan of numbering each play, but the method of calling a certain number to the attention of the players is accomplished in many different ways. One way which is quite commonly used is to add the first two numbers given. If this system is used, the plays should be numbered from ten upwards, because there are so few combinations of numbers which can be added to indicate a small number, while above ten many combinations of two numbers can be added which will result in the number desired; for instance, the number of the play which the quarter-back has decided to use is 12. The first two numbers he calls out can be 7-5, 5-7, 8-4, 4-8, 9-3, 3-9, 10-2, 2-10, 11-1, 1-11, etc. It is not necessary to use the first two numbers in using this system—it can be understood that the second and third numbers are to be added, or the first and third.

Another system used by many prominent teams is to have the plays numbered from ten upward, and indicate the number by having the players form it by taking the second digit of the first number called for the first digit of the number of the play, and the first digit of the second number called to indicate the second digit of the number of the play; for instance, if the number of the play wished to be indicated is 15, the quarter calls out the numbers 21-57-33, etc. If he decides to use play number 21, he can call out the numbers 42-17-26, etc. This method of giving the signals need not be worked in exactly the manner described above; it can be understood that the second digits of the first two numbers are to form the signal number, and then 32-16-11, etc. would indicate the number 26.

Another plan for indicating the number of the play is to have a key number, and have it understood that the number following a number with the key number in it will be the number of the play; for example, let 6 be the key number, and 14 the number desired to be indicated; the quarter-back would then call out 25-36-14-27, etc., and the players would easily understand the signal. He might also call out 62-14-37, etc., and indicate the same play, since the key number, 6, is contained in the first number called.

The simplest method of all, to use in indicating the number of the play, is to have it understood that the signal number is to be the first number called, or the second number; or it may be the third number, whichever is decided upon. Either this method, or the one where a key number is used, I believe to be better than the others mentioned, because of their simplicity. There should be no thought or mental calculation necessary on the part of the players in figuring out the signal number, because no matter how simple the calculation may be, it will draw the players' attention away from the game for an instant or more, and interfere with their playing. The signal number should be conveyed to them in the simplest manner possible, so that they instantly catch it, and can devote their whole thought to the game and their part in the play, as soon as the signal is given. Many teams make their system of signals too complicated, seeming to fear that the opponents will be able to figure out the plays if the signals are simple, when as a matter of fact, even the very simplest signals will only seldom be fathomed by opposing players. During the first two or three seasons in which I coached the Indians, the plays were numbered and the first number called was the signal number, and yet with a system so simple as that, no team, as far as I could judge, ever figured out the Indians' signals.

Very often the statement is made that a team "caught on" to the other team's signals during or before the game, but it is very probable, in nearly every such case, that some player or players indicated the direction of the plays by their actions or looks, or the quarter-back, in giving the signals, may have emphasized the signal number, and by repeatedly doing this, and using a few good plays quite often, the opponents may have been able to diagnose certain plays. Whenever it is feared that the opponents may have solved the signals, a change can be quickly made at any time, if the system is a simple one and the plays are numbered; for example, if the second number has been the signal number, it can easily be changed to the third or fourth without bothering the players at all. In fact they should be accustomed to several different methods of giving the signals, because in their practice games with the second team, the latter should not know where the play is coming every time a signal is called.

The signals should be mastered thoroughly, and practiced until every player knows instinctively, the instant he hears a signal, just what he is to do in the play. The substitutes should know them as perfectly as the regulars, so that when one of them is called upon, the team will not be slowed up, or the team work interfered with.

It is usual to number the plays so that even-numbered ones are aimed at one side of the line, while the odd-numbered plays are directed to the other. This aids in simplifying matters, and if any player does not happen to remember the play, he will at least know upon which side of the line the play is to be directed.

STARTING SIGNALS

Quite a number of teams use starting signals when in possession of the ball, in order that the players may not have to wait for the ball to be snapped as their signal to start. When such a signal is well conceived and properly worked up, it is a great advantage, because it enables the whole team to get off *with* the ball instead of an instant after it is snapped. This is especially advantageous for the line-men, because it gives them an instant's start on their opponents, who are watching the snap of the ball for their signal to charge, and therefore the linemen of the team using the starting signal when they have the ball, "get the charge" upon their opponents. Another advantage to be gained by it is that the players do not necessarily have to be in a position where they can see the ball.

Unless such a signal is well planned and thoroughly mastered, it is likely to prove a hindrance instead of an advantage, because it may seriously interfere with the team work, on account of the players getting off raggedly, or the ball being passed at the wrong time, and it would not be wise for the smaller teams to attempt such advanced and complicated tactics.

The simplest starting signal is to have it understood that the players will start, and the ball will be passed, upon the fourth number called, or it may be the fifth number; but this is so simple that the opponents will soon be able to judge when the ball is to be snapped as well as the team having the ball, and then the advantage of the signal is lost. If a key number is used in giving the signals, the fault in the starting signal above described can be overcome, because the starting signal can then be the third or fourth number after the number of the play, and as the key number may be the first, second, or third number called, the starting signal will not always come in the same place, and the opponents will not be able to solve it.

If it is arranged to have the play signal the first, the second, or the third number called, a key number can be used to indicate that the start will be made upon the second digit of the number following the key number; for example, we will suppose that the second number is the number of the play, and 4 is the key number for the starting signal; then the quarter-back may call 11-17-23-34-56, and the players will understand that the play is 17, and that the ball will be snapped and all will start on 6—the second digit of the number following the key number, 4.

If, in the system used, the signal number is determined by adding the first two numbers, or by using certain digits of the first two numbers, the starting signal can be the signal number itself. Since the players must get this number from the first two numbers called in order to know what play is to be used, it is impressed upon their minds, and no further mental effort is required to determine the starting signal. As an example, we will assume that the second digits of the first two numbers will indicate the number of the play, and 19 is the play desired to be used; the quarter will then call 21-39-12-6-19, and the team will start as soon as they hear "nineteen." This number can be the fourth, fifth, or sixth number, so that the starting signal will not come in a certain place, and the opponents will not be able to solve it.

Only a few plans for starting signals are given, but some of them will work well, and those explained will, no doubt, suggest others to anyone who will study the matter.

No team, whose players have had experience and are well coached, need be without the aid of such a signal, but as mentioned before, a starting signal which does not work perfectly is a handicap rather than a help, and school boys and teams composed of inexperienced players should not try to work it up.

Generalship.

UNDER this head it is intended to treat, not only of the generalship with which an important game should be handled, but of the intelligent management of the whole season's campaign.

THE SCHEDULE

The schedule is generally arranged with the idea of providing the team with practice games early in the season, these games increasing in importance as the season progresses, and leading up to one or two final championship games which are made the climax of the season, and for which nearly every other game is considered as a means of development and preparation.

The strongest teams, as a rule, try to arrange their schedules so that the games will be comparatively easy at the start, and harder as the season advances, but with the idea of reaching the final championship game or games without a defeat. The weaker teams very often arrange their early games with stronger teams out of their class, realizing that they will almost surely be beaten, but with the idea of giving the players practice and experience which will aid them later in the season in their championship games with teams in their own class.

Occasionally a supposedly minor team will be blessed with unusually good material; which will get together early, and by developing quickly, try to surprise a so-called "big" team which has scheduled an early practice game with them. If the minor team happens to win such a game, it gives the players some temporary glory and notoriety, but usually results in disaster before the end of the season, by reason of overconfidence or 'swelled head," and overtraining because of getting into top-notch condition too soon. While it is a laudable desire for every team to win all the games possible, the success of the season will usually be greater if the early games are considered as practice games pure and ismple, and no special preparation made for them. The games later in the season are usually the ones upon which the standing of the team, or the success of the season, is based, and these should be the contests to be borne in mind throughout the season, and gradually worked up to. In doing this, the other games should not be overlooked by any means, nor played without putting forth every effort, and making such careful preparation as will not interfere with the steady and gradual development of the team.

Some schedules are arranged in such a manner that a very important game has to be played in the middle of the season and another at the end. With such a schedule, the team is usually developed rather early, and put in prime condition for the midseason game, after which it is easily handled for a week or two, and then developed for the second, or final climax. A team which has a schedule arranged in this manner will very seldom play in top notch form in both of these games, and unless it is an unusually strong one, is almost sure to be beaten in one of them. With a schedule like this, it will prove to be good generalship to regard the final game as the most important, and not have the team in top notch for the midseason contest. It will be wise to follow both suggestions, because if the midseason game should be won without being in top notch form, but with the idea that it was of more importance than the final contest, overconfidence and lack of interest would then ruin the team's chances in the latter.

About the poorest schedule a team can have is one in which the most important game comes about the middle of the season, and closing with a game of minor importance. A team with such an arrangement of games may do well in the early season, and in its important game, but is almost sure to deteriorate and spoil its reputation in the latter part of the season, by reason of overconfidence, and lack of interest and enthusiasm.

No matter how the schedule is arranged, it should be the aim of every team to make gradual and steady improvement as the season progresses. If defeats come, everything possible should be done to keep the players from becoming disheartened, and the defects in the team's play which caused the defeats should be pointed out to the players and corrected. No schedule should be arranged which will necessitate playing more than half the games with teams known to be stronger than the team for which it is arranged, because nothing will so dishearten the players as several successive defeats. One or two defeats, early or in the middle of the season, usually aid in developing a team, because they bring out the weak points and keep the players in a receptive mood for coaching. It is just as great a mistake to arrange a schedule which is too easy as it is to make it too hard. If the practice games, leading to the final game or games, are all with teams of a minor class and easily won, the championship games will be reached without having had a chance to properly test the players or the plays. Some players will appear to excellent advantage in the minor games, but will be found wanting when up against strong opponents, and many plays, which work well against weaker teams, will be found worthless in games where the teams are evenly matched; therefore every team should have some games with worthy opponents before their championship games are reached, in order that the fainthearted or easily rattled players, and the unsuccessful plays may be weeded out.

THE MATERIAL.

Good judgment, or generalship, should be exercised in handling the material and in placing the players in the positions for which they are best fitted. No matter how good the backs may be, they cannot accomplish much behind a weak line, while mediocre backs will be able to get good results behind a strong line; therefore it is of first importance to so arrange the players as to provide a strong line. As a rule, it will be found that the inexperienced candidates, provided they have sufficient weight, will be able to do better work as guards, or at center, than in any other positions, because experience and knowledge of the game are not so necessary for the three center men. A player who has had considerable experience as a guard can easily learn to play tackle; and as a rule, a player who has learned to play tackle can be developed into a good end, provided he has enough of speed; therefore a good rule to follow, in arranging the players in the line, is to place the inexperienced men in the three center positions, and move out the experienced ones, placing those with the greatest experience and most ability at the ends.

In choosing a quarterback the liveliest, coolest, and headiest player among the candidates should be picked out, whether he has had experience in playing the position or not. Such a player will easily learn the duties of a quarterback, and be able to render better service here than anywhere else upon the team. Without a quarterback who is a general and a leader, in whom the other players have the utmost confidence, no team will be able to get satisfactory results.

The heaviest of the backfield material should, as a rule, be placed in the position of full-back, and in selecting all of the backs, their defensive ability should be considered just as important as their ability to advance the ball. Every team should have at least two good punters and a field goal kicker in its makeup, although these need not necessarily be backs.

Left-handed and left-footed players are better suited to positions upon the right side of the line than upon the left.

The man who has the handling and the selection of the material in charge must be a general, as he has all kinds of temperaments to deal with and will be confronted with many situations and difficulties, which must be handled with tact and diplomacy. He must show no favoritism, and should endeavor, by all means, to keep the players in good humor, and free from jealousies and ill-feeling toward each other. Harmony should be the watchword of the season, because no combination of individuals working together for a common purpose, can secure the best results unless they pull together, and this is especially true of a football team.

PLANNING THE CAMPAIGN

In preparing for all except the early practice games, a study should be made of the systems of offense and defense relied upon by the opponents, so that the players may be instructed as to the best method of meeting them. The plays may have to be changed slightly from week to week, in order to cope with different styles of defense, while the formations and plays relied upon by opposing teams will necessitate changes in the regular system of defense. It is a good plan to have the scrub, or second team play as nearly as possible the same style of game in the practice games of the week that will be used by the team which will be met on Saturday.

Having learned how to meet different systems or styles of play as the season progresses, the players will be ready to meet most any situation in the final games, and not be rendered helpless by having something new sprung upon them.

A special study should be made of the style of game played by the team or teams with whom the championship games are to be played, and the whole season should be centered upon these games. While the other games should be prepared for and played with determination and spirit, they should be regarded as of minor importance, and every effort put forth to instill in the players the importance of the championship game or games, and an intense desire and determination to fairly overcome their rivals.

The mental attitude of the players toward the opponents or the games plays a very important part in the result of many games. No team will do its best if the players go into a game without a full realization that they will have to put forth their best efforts to win or are overconfident; and very often under such conditions the unlooked-for strength and determination of the opponents will so surprise, daze, and demoralize a team that the game results in a disastrous defeat, which might have been avoided if the players had gone into the game with the right spirit.

THE GAME.

During the week preceding a championship game the team should be handled very carefully. If there are any players suffering from injuries, they should not engage in any rough exercise, and the practice of the week should be devoted to smoothing up the plays and perfecting the team work.

If the game is to be played away from home, but within a two or three hours' ride, the trip will interfere less with the players if taken upon the morning of the day of the game than if taken the day before, because the players will rest better in their own beds, and will not be so affected by nervous excitement as they would be in a strange place, near the scene of the struggle. Where the game is to be played more than a hundred miles from home, the trip should be made the day before, and if possible arranged so that the destination will be reached during the afternoon or evening. The journey, if not too long, will just tire the players enough to make them sleep well. It is not a good plan to make the trip to the place where the game is to be played two or three days ahead, as the excitement prevailing in the locality, and the change of surroundings and food, are likely to have an injurious effect upon the players.

The team should be prepared with an outfit suitable for any kind of weather conditions, especial attention being given to the shoes and the cleats upon them. If the field is muddy, or if it rainy, the suits should be light and the cleats upon the shoes long. If the weather is very cold, it will be advantageous for the players to wear warm underwear.

Before tossing for the choice of the goal or the kick-off, the direction of the wind and the position of the sun should be noted, and also the tendency of the wind to increase or diminish late in the afternoon. In some localities the wind diminishes as night approaches, and in this case the winner of the toss should choose the goal favored by the wind; whereas, if the wind is likely to increase toward evening, the choice should be made so as to get the benefit of the wind in the last period.

When a team receives the kick-off with a favored wind, or a wind blowing across the field, good generalship on the part of the opposing team should cause it to place the kick-off to the side or corner of the field least favored, or to the windward side. If successful in so placing the kick, the team receiving it (provided it is run back straight ahead from the point where the ball is caught) will be forced, when it punts, to kick the ball across the path of the wind to keep it from going out of bounds; while if the ball was kicked off to the other side, the ball could be returned by a punt diagonally across the field with the wind almost behind it. It is usually good generalship, in any case, for the kick-off to be placed to the side because the best man to run the ball back is usually placed directly in front of the goal, and it is wise to kick the ball where he cannot get it. It is also more difficult for the receiving team to get together and form interference at one side of the field than in the center, and the team kicking off can place its best tacklers, and an extra man or two, upon the side toward which the kick-off is to be made.

A football game is very similar, in many respects, to a war, and good generalship is as important in one as in the other. Each scrimmage represents a battle, in which the opposing forces are lined up opposite each other, one side defending itself against the attack of the other. The lines represent the infantry, and the backs can be likened to cavalry, quick moving, and able to charge the enemy at any spot, or rush to the support of any position attacked. The quarterback or general of the side making the attack should study well the defense of the enemy, and decide whether to force through their center, turn their flank by a quick movement, deceive them with a fake movement in one direction while the real attack is made at another spot, or transfer the battle to a more favorable locality by a punt. In making this decision, he should take into consideration the condition of the field, the direction of the wind, and especially the position on the field, with reference to the goal or side lines, and the number of the down and the distance to be gained. If the wind is favorable, and the ball is near the goal line which his team is defending, the battle should by all means be transferred to the enemy's territory by a punt, reserving ammunition and strength for the attack when an opportunity is gained within striking distance of the enemy's goal.

As a rule the ball should be punted out of a team's territory unless there is an adverse wind, in which case it is usually better to retain the ball until forced to punt. Upon fourth down, unless near the opponents' goal, the ball should be punted or forward passed when there is not a reasonable certainty that the required distance for a first down can be gained, and this should amount to almost absolute certainty where the team in possession of the ball is in its own territory.

If a team is able to hold the opponents and prevent their gaining, it is wise to punt often, especially if the team excels in a punting game; but where the opponents are the stronger, and able to make consistent gains when rushing the ball, the weaker team should retain the ball as long as possible whenever they gain possession of it, and only punt when forced to do so upon fourth down, because so long as the ball is kept away from their opponents, the latter are unable to make much headway or score. Such tactics are also advisable when a team has a lead and is content to keep the other side from overtaking them, as it is very discouraging for a losing team, only a few points behind, to realize that the time is fast slipping away, and that they may be unable to get a chance to use their plays and score before the whistle blows.

When rushing the ball, the quarter should choose one of the strongest plays for use upon the first down—one which is usually good for five or more yards, and generally such plays should be directed outside of tackle. If the defense of the opponents is scattered, it may be advisable to send the first play through the line, but usually it is not wise to depend upon gaining ten yards in four downs by bucking the line. If four or more yards are gained upon the first trial, the remaining distance necessary for a first down can usually be secured by straight plays which can be depended upon for steady and sure gains. If the play used upon first down is unsuccessful, an end run or a trick play should be used upon the second down, and if this is stopped without much gain, a forward pass, trick play or a strong play outside of tackle should be resorted to upon the third down.

On fourth down, unless practically certain of gaining the required distance, the ball should be punted unless it is near enough to the opponents goal for a field goal trial. A forward pass would be the proper play on fourth down near the opponent's goal and on the side of the field where a field goal would be difficult.

Good generalship is as necessary upon the part of the players, and especially upon the part of the captain, when the team is upon the defence, as when rushing the ball. By studying the situation upon every down, noting the distance to be gained and the part of the gridiron where the ball is situated, the defensive players can determine pretty closely what sort of tactics will be used upon nearly every play. The backs particularly should be able to size up what play to be on the lookout for and change their positions accordingly, closing in when expecting a line attack and moving back when a punt, a forward pass, or a trick play is likely to be pulled off. If the field and the ball are slippery, the defense should play in much closer than upon a dry day, because end runs and fancy plays will be impossible under these conditions, and the main strength of the attack will very likely consist of plays directed at the line.

All the defects in the team's play can be noted during the first period and corrected during the intermission, and the team which is in the hands of the best general, whether he be captain or coach, will usually show the greatest improvement as the game progresses.

This shows correct position of the players upon regular formation ready for the ball to be snapped, except that the quarter should have his hands extended toward the ball, instead of upon his knees.

Offense.

EVERY team's offense should consist of a limited number of first class plays, perfectly mastered, and of sufficient variety to enable it to meet any style of defense under all sorts of conditions, and be able to take advantage of any weakness which might develop in the defense of opposing teams. No team should depend upon one style of attack. The offensive strength should consist of straight, powerful line plays, end runs with perfectly formed interference, two or three fake plays which have some power in them, and do not depend entirely upon deceiving the opponents, two or three good forward pass plays, and several plays from the punt formation. These should be combined with ability to kick field goals, and a quick punt from a regular running formation is often of value and should occasionally be used when the ball can be punted over the defensive fullback's head.

Under the rules now in vogue the tendency is to do away with the quarter-back passing the ball and the ball will be passed by many teams directly from center to runner. There will also be a tendency to use more open formation plays because, not being permitted to push or pull, the backs must now go ahead of the runner and form protection for him and open up a passage through the line as well as around the ends. The forward pass will be more used than in the past few years, because of the removal of some of its restrictions, protecting the receiver of it, and lessening the penalty when it is not properly played.

Many teams are unwisely taught a large number of plays—so many that it is impossible to master them all thoroughly, and often resulting in confusion of signals. It is much better to have a few good plays well learned, than to have a large assortment imperfectly worked up and some of which are likely to be of doubtful strength. The more important and harder the game the fewer plays are used, because the team has the ball less, has to punt more, and when rushing the ball only uses a select few of its strongest plays.

Trick plays are useful to add variety of the atack, to keep the opponents guessing and thus aid the regular plays, and occasionally to pull off a long run, but they should not be depended upon to win games, and only a few good ones should be taught the players.

In diagraming the following plays, care has been taken to select only those which are sure to be good ones. Many more might be explained, but the list here diagramed is large enough, and varied enough, to enable any team to select from it a powerful, scientific and varied attack, which will succeed against the defense of any team in its class.

The plays are diagramed upon five-yard squares, so that the approximate distance can be seen at a glance, and each play is only diagramed for one side of the line. How the same play should be played on the opposite side, can easily be figured out by studying the diagrams, or by copying the plays upon a thin sheet of paper, holding to the light, and looking at the reverse side. The man who carries the ball is indicated by the solid black circle. The defensive back, who plays in the extreme back-field to handle punts, etc., is not shown in the diagrams.

There are eight plays diagramed for one side of the line from the regular formation, or sixteen in all; fourteen diagrams, or twenty-eight plays from the backs-over formation; five diagrams, or ten plays from the open formation; eight diagrams or sixteen plays from the punt formation, and eight diagrams or sixteen plays from the backs in line quick shift formation. This furnishes a total of eighty-six selected plays, without counting the punt, drop-kick, or quick place-kick. Twenty good plays are enough for any team, and no team should have over twenty-five.

The regular simple formation plays and the punts should be given the team as early as possible, and the forward passes and other plays should then be mastered at the rate of about two or three each week.

My advice would be to use only two or three of the formations from which the following plays are described. The plays from the regular formation, backs over direct pass formation and punt formation would make a very good system of offense, and the plays from the backs in line quick shift formation together with the punt formation plays would also provide an excellent attack.

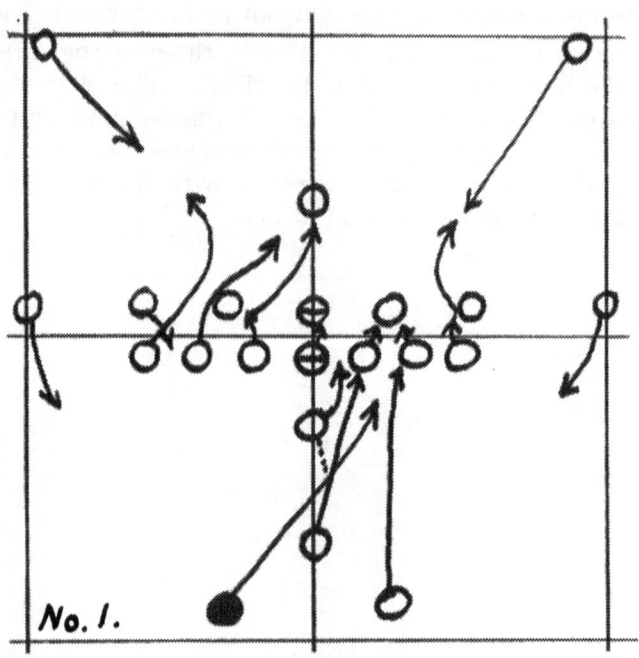

REGULAR FORMATION

No. 1. This play is designed to go through the opposing guard, or between him and the tackle. Quarter passes the ball to left half-back who carries the ball as indicated behind interference formed by the fullback and right half-back. The guard and tackle carry the opposing guard back and to the left, while the right end throws the opposing tackle out. If the opposing guard plays close to his center so that the guard can handle him alone the tackle can then aid the end in disposing of the opposing tackle. The quarter advances into the line as indicated to help bend the line back. All the line men should go through and block the secondary defense after putting their opposing line men out of the play.

95

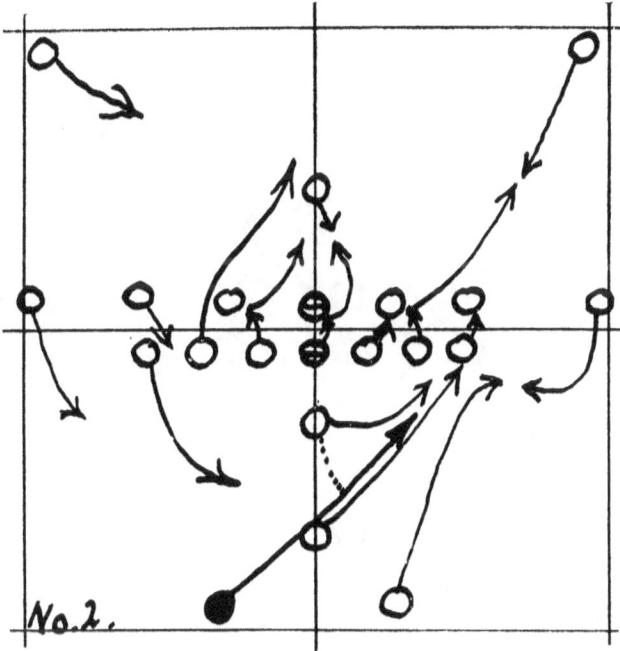

No. 2. This is a mass upon tackle or a straight-off-tackle play. Left half-back takes the ball behind the quarter, full-back and right half-back. The play should be aimed just outside your own right end. Right half runs shoulder to shoulder with his full-back and then dives into the opposing end and throws him out just as he comes in to tackle. Right half should not run out and toward the end, but close in as indicated, so that he will be sure to be in position to block the end out. If the opposing left guard is playing wide the tackle will have to help his guard take care of him, but if he is playing close to center the tackle can help his end put the opposing tackle out of the play and go through to block the secondary defense. Left end comes around to make the play safe.

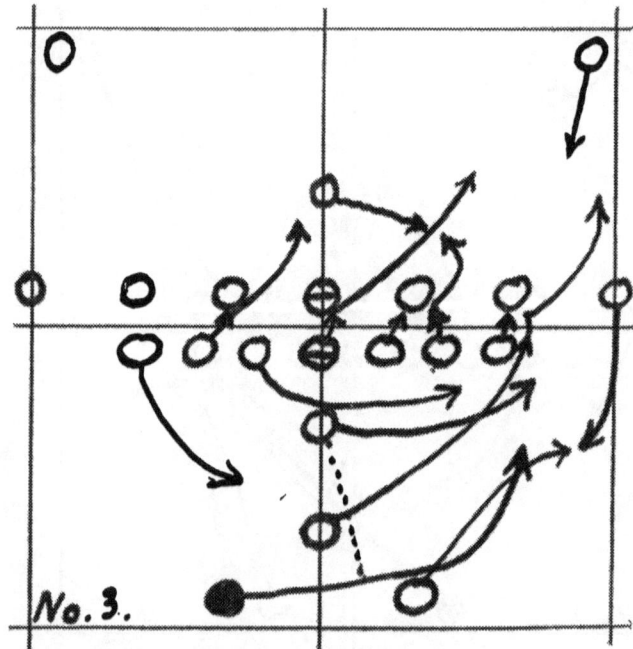

No. 3. Short end run aimed to go between opposing tackle and end. In this play the left half should start as for a wide end run so as to allow his interference plenty of time to form and to bring the opposing end pretty well out, so that right half can block him out just as the runner turns in. Full back helps the end block the opposing tackle and then blocks defensive left half. Right tackle helps the guard if his opponent plays very wide, otherwise he helps his end block the tackle. Left guard and quarter get into the interference, and left end follows up the play to guard against a fumble and to keep opponents from tackling from behind. Other linemen block as indicated and go through to cut off the secondary defense.

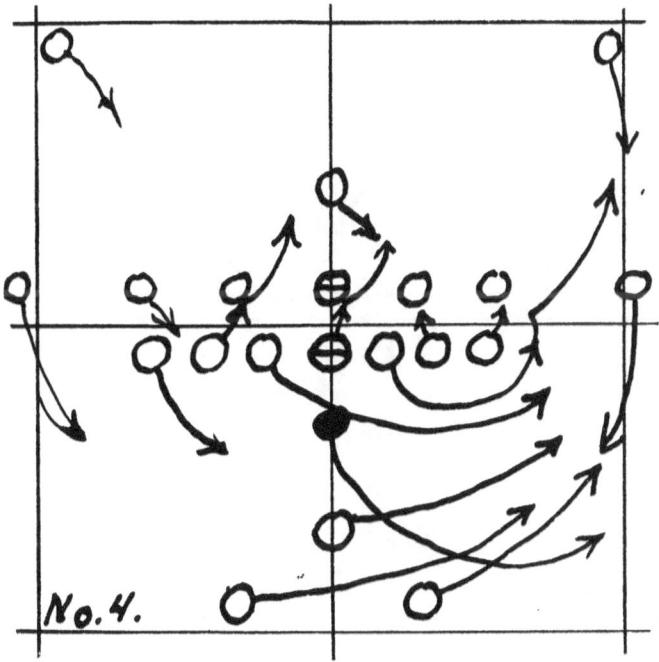

No. 4. Wide quarter back run. In this play both full back and right half should dispose of the opposing left end, and left half should also take him if he eludes the other interference. Both guards can get into the interference in this play and they are an important factor in its success. The quarter starts pretty well back and should get off with a lot of speed being careful not to run too close to the line. **After he gets started he should look for openings and turn straight down the field as soon as an opening presents itself.** Left end comes around to look after fumbles and to protect the runner from behind.

98

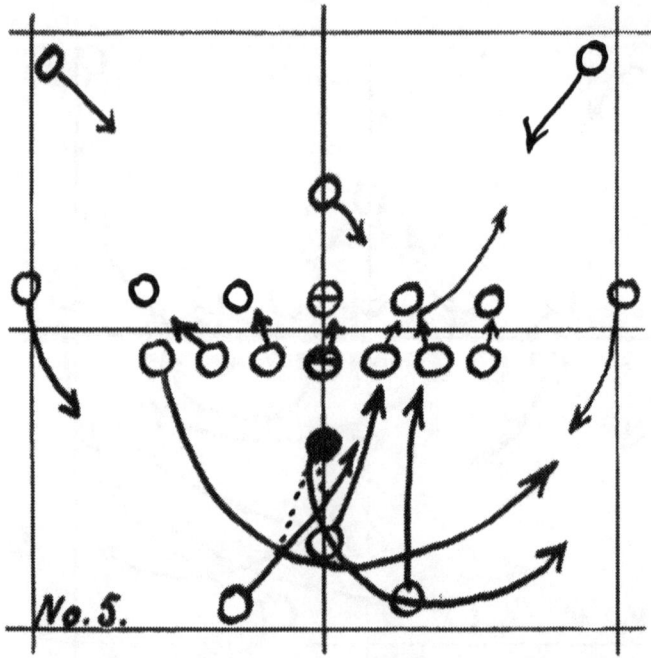

No. 5. This is a fake line attack and double pass quarter-back run. The play starts off exactly as No. 1. Quarter passes the ball to left half and stands with his back to center. Left half hands quarter the ball as he passes and the quarter starts pretty wide coming out behind his left end, who leaves his position with the snap of the ball and comes around as interference for the quarter, putting the opposing left end out of the play. Left tackle helps block momentarily and then goes through and blocks defensive left half. This is an excellent play with a fast quarter if properly played and made to look like No. 1 when it starts off.

Another good play could be made to work with this by having the right end block momentarily and then run wide and the quarter make a forward pass to the end after running back five yards.

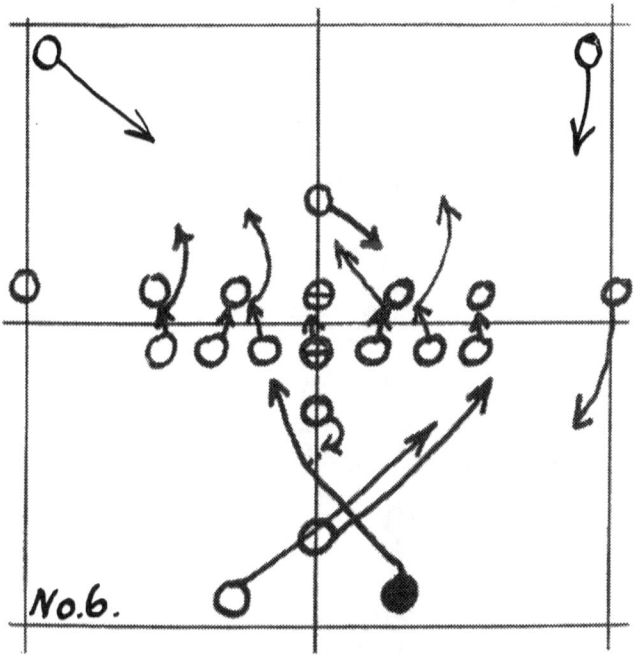

No. 6. This is a delayed pass or split play which works well. The play is made to look like No. 2. The left half makes a bluff to take the ball from the quarter who turns to the right and makes a fake pass to him. Right half lays low, perhaps taking one step to the right, and then shoots to the left as the other backs have passed. The hole should be made either between guard and center, or guard and tackle, whichever works best, and the right half should be on the alert to take the opening wherever it is.

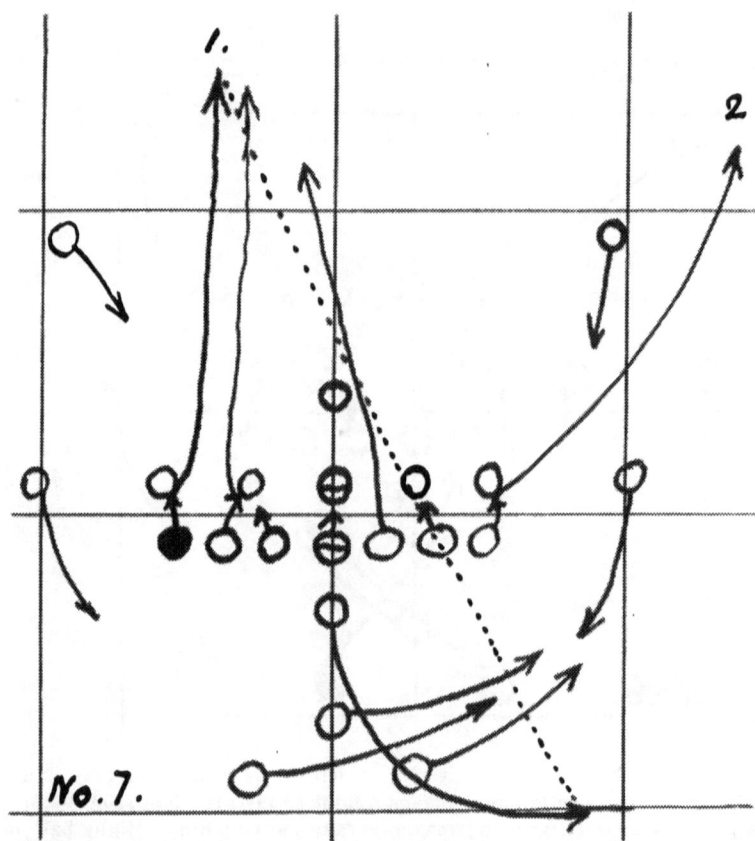

No. 7. Forward pass. This play starts off as a quarter-back run similar to No. 4, except that the linemen do not get into the interference. Quarter comes back and runs wide and far enough to allow his left end to get well down the field. He then passes the ball to left end if the latter is free, but he can also pass to right end, or continue running with the ball if both ends are covered. It may work better for the left end to run farther out to the left in this play, and the quarter must remember to run far enough back so that the pass is made at least five yards behind the line.

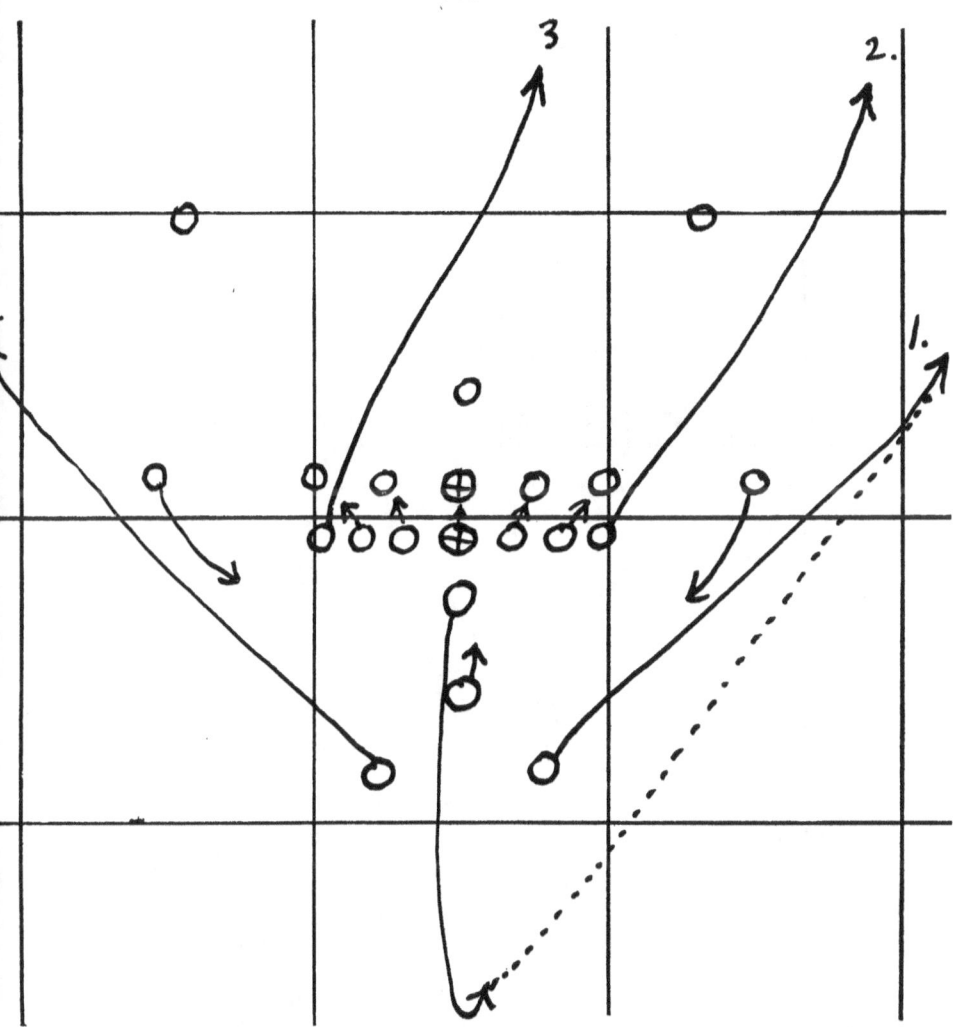

No. 8. An excellent forward pass. Players numbered 1, 2, 3, and 4 run quickly upon the snap of the ball as indicated. Fullback holds his position and protects quarter back, who gets the ball from center and runs quickly back from five to ten yards and then turns and passes the ball to No. 1, 2, 3, or 4. Probably the pass will work better on No. 1, because the secondary defense will very likely be drawn away from him to cover No. 2 and 3. The latter players should look around and be ready in case the ball is thrown to either of them. If opposing left end follows No. 1 out, the quarter can continue running to the right until the end comes after him.

ADDITIONAL PLAYS from the regular formation can be worked up as follows: For a short sure gain the quarter can take the ball and dive straight through center, the quarter can pass the ball to the fullback for a quick plunge through either side of center or to either halfback for quick plunges straight ahead through quick openings between guard and tackle. These are all good for sure small gains and so simple that they need not be diagramed.

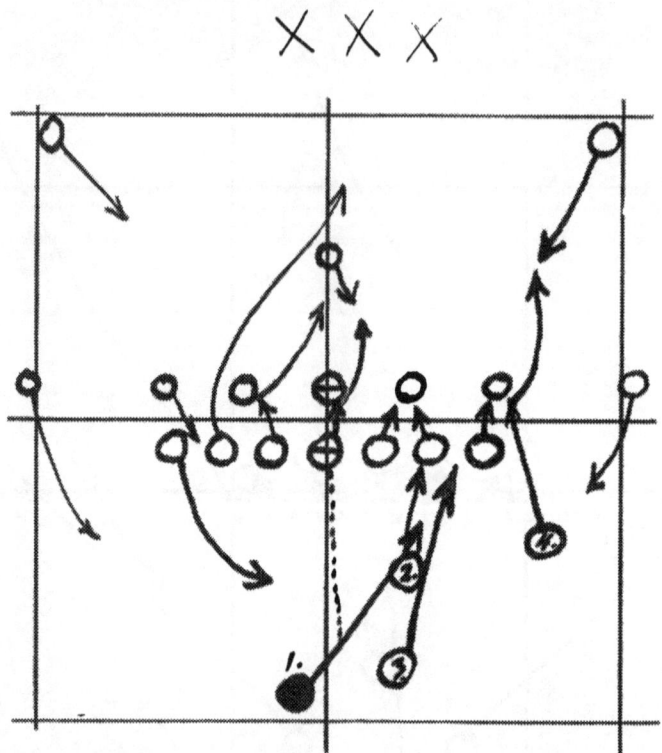

BACKS OVER, DIRECT PASS FORMATION

No. 9. This play and those following up to No. 16, are from a direct pass formation in which the backs are massed upon one side of the ball. Left half stands back about four and a half to five yards from the line and behind the hole between his left guard and center. No. 3 stands slightly closer to the line and back of right guard. No. 2 stands about two and a half yards back of the line and behind the opening between right guard and right tackle. No. 4 stands outside of his right end and about a yard and a half to two yards back but he can move closer or up to the line if the opposing tackle plays very wide so that right end has trouble in blocking him.

In this play left half takes the ball on a direct pass and carries it behind No. 2 and 3 between the opposing left guard and tackle, No. 4 helps block tackle and goes on to cut off defensive left half. Left end comes around to make the play safe.

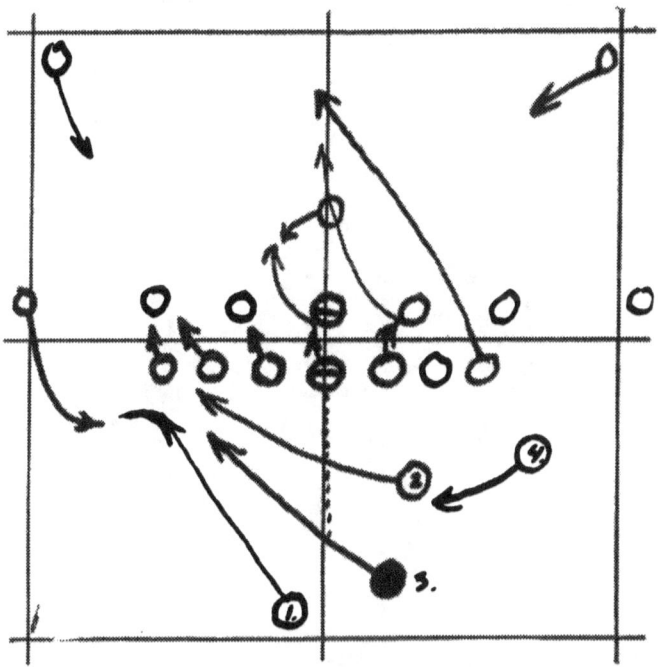

No. 10. This is a play to the weak side just off tackle. No. 5 takes the ball on a direct pass with Nos. 2 and 1 to interfere for him. No. 1 runs close in and then dives into and forces the defensive end out as he comes in to tackle. No 4 makes the play safe and the line men block or go through to cut off secondary defense as indicated.

If play No. 19 is used substitute play No. 17 for the above play.

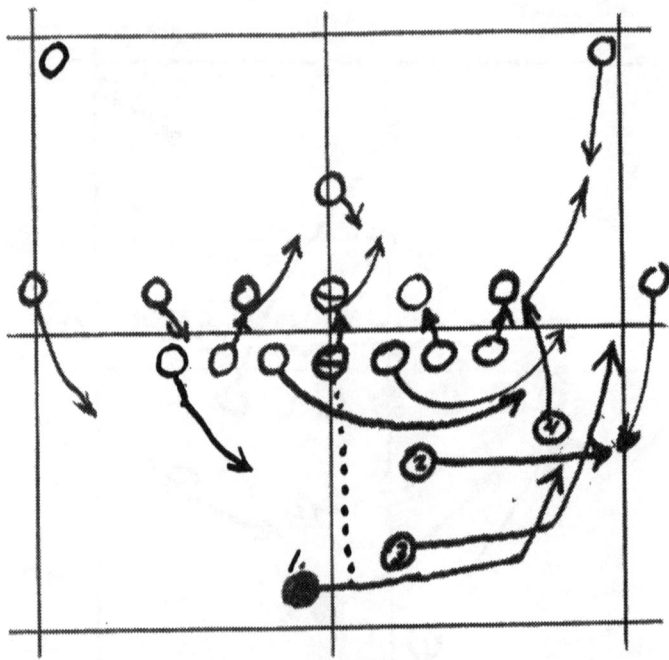

No. 11. Short end run. No. 2 blocks the defensive end out. No. 4 helps block the defensive tackle and then takes the defensive half. No. 1 carries the ball and follows No. 3, running wide for three or four yards as if to circle the end and then cutting in quickly as No. 2 blocks the end out. Both guards leave their positions with the snap of the ball and come around in the interference in which they form an effective part. Left tackle and center block as indicated and then go through to cut off secondary defense. Left end follows up the play to recover possible fumble and to protect the runner from behind. This is a very effective ground gainer.

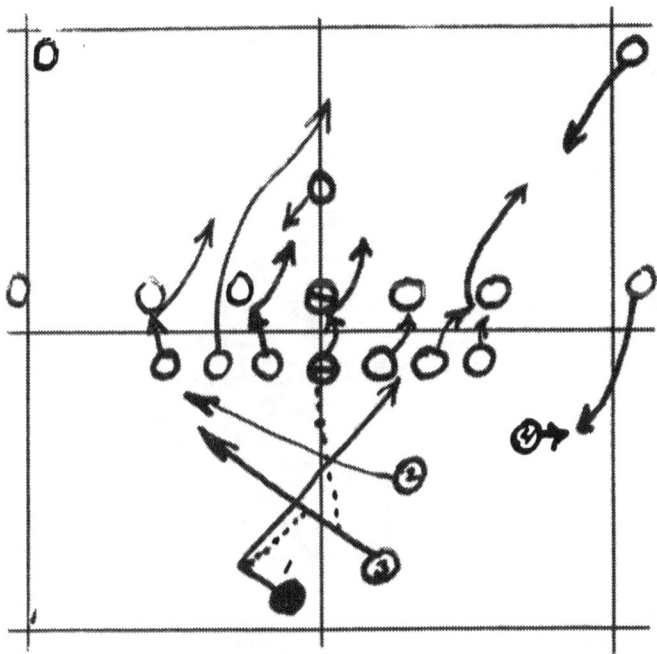

No. 12. Fake tackle play and delayed pass. This play is made to look like No. 10, No. 3 taking the ball and passing to No. 1 as he passes him. No. 1 takes one step with his left foot, keeping close to the ground, and, after securing the ball, carries it between opponent's left guard and left tackle. No. 1 should be careful not to run from his position but take one step to the left, stop, get the ball and then run from that point. The taking of but one step and then a complete stop is necessary to enable the back to turn sharply before getting too close to the line.

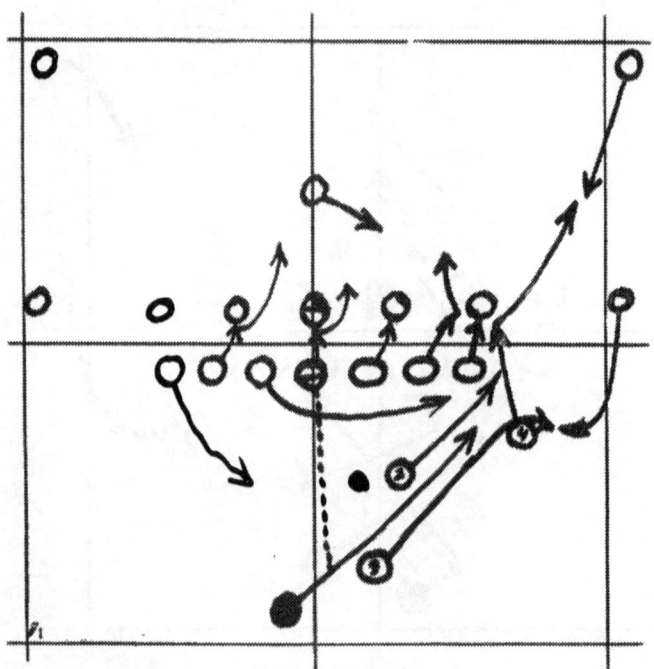

No. 13. Mass upon tackle. This play is aimed to just slide off the opposing tackle. No. 4 helps drive the tackle back and then blocks defensive half. No. 1 takes the ball behind No. 2, and left guard protects him from the side. No. 3 runs close to No. 2, so as to be sure to be inside the defensive end and then blocks the latter out as he comes in to tackle the runner.

107

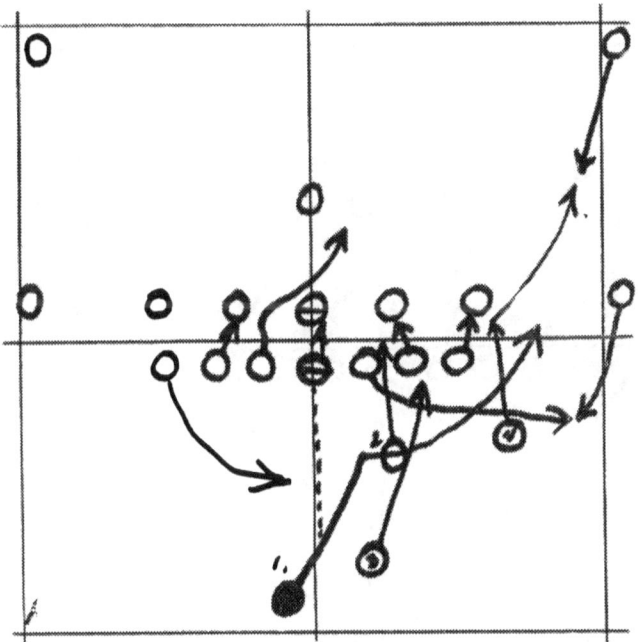

No. 14. This play starts off and is made to look like No. 9. The right guard leaves his position with the snap of the ball and goes out to block the defensive end. Coming from so close to the line the latter will not notice him until too late. No. 2 shoots into the hole left vacant by the guard. No. 3 runs for the hole the other side of his right tackle. No. 1 takes the ball and advances two or three short steps slightly to the right of center and then turns sharply and speedily to the right, just going outside of tackle. This is a very deceiving and effective play if played properly. No. 1 should be careful not to start so fast that he cannot turn quickly before getting too close to the line.

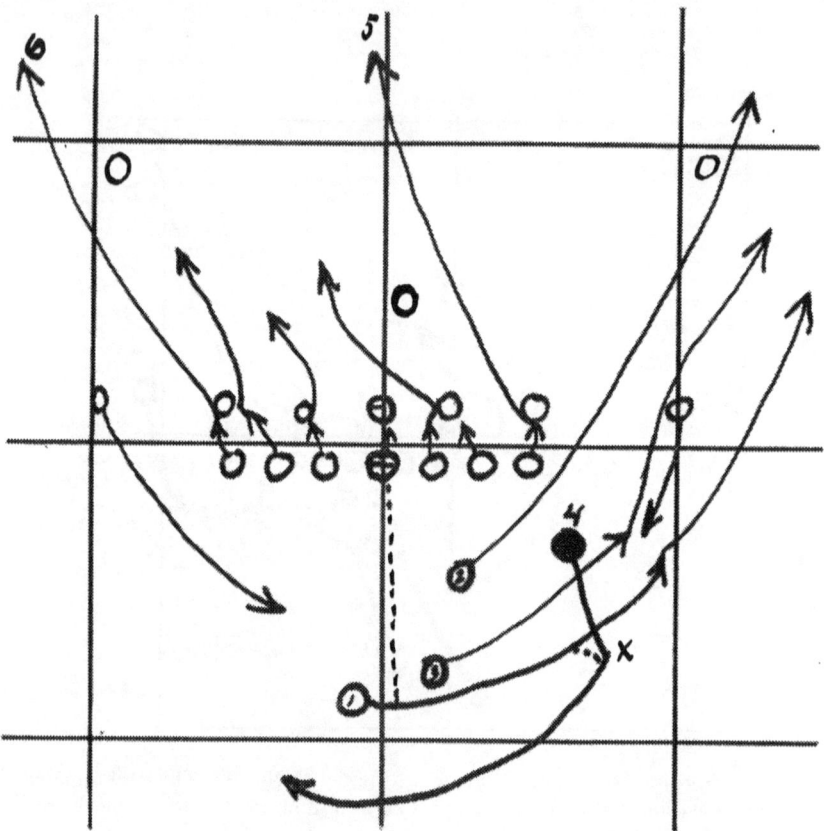

No. 15. Criss-cross forward pass or run. No. 4 backs up when the ball is snapped, keeping low and not starting to run until he secures the ball from No. 1, who runs with it as though for a run around right end. As No. 1 passes No. 4 he places the ball against the latter's stomach. No. 4 should at that time be at X and facing in the direction he is to run. He should run well back and to the left, after securing the ball, and if he sees that the opponent's right end has overrun him he can continue the play as a run. If he sees that he is likely to be intercepted he can pass the ball to No. 6, No. 5, or across to No. 1, 2 or 3. Probably No. 6 will be best man to pass to. The runner must run far enough back so as to elude opposing right end and to have time to make the pass at least five yards back of the line.

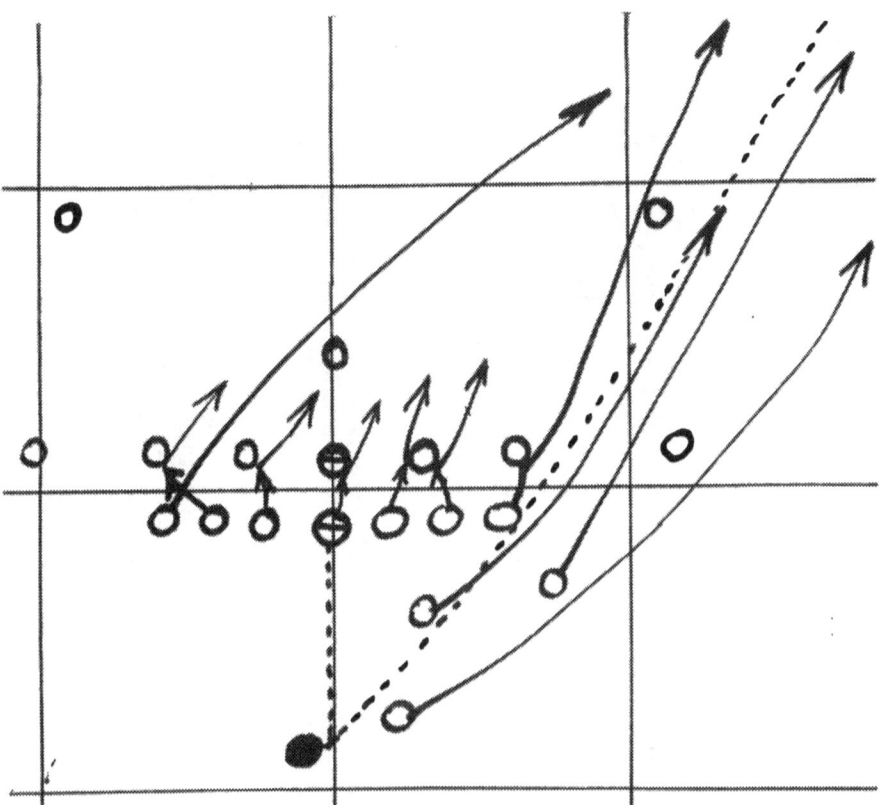

No. 16. This is a quick punt which can be used for the purpose of punting over the defensive full back's head if he comes up closer to the scrimmage line than he should. The ends and backs charge down the field with the snap of the ball. The punter should step backward a yard or two while recovering the ball from center and he can start to run with it a few steps before punting. This makes the play more effective because it gives the ends and backs more time to get down the field and it also takes more time for the defence to diagnose the play. This diagram is slightly wrong, as the punter must be five or more yards back of the line when the punt is made.

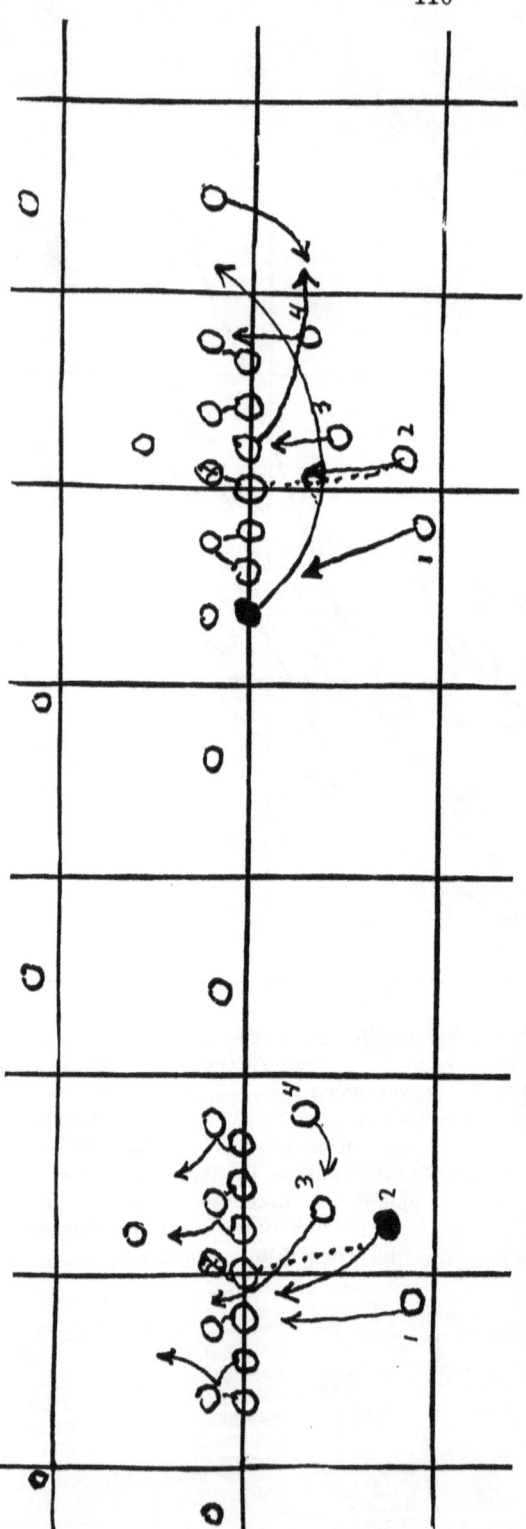

No. 17—With this formation the defending center is likely to shift opposite the opening between the right guard, while the opposing right guard is not likely to move in towards center. In these positions it is easy for left guard and center to open a hole in the opponent's line. The pass is direct to No. 2. No. 3 goes hard and low ahead of the man with the ball. No. 1 advances by the side of No. 2 and helps bend the line back in case there is no opening. No. 4 backs up the play, guarding against a fumble. The line men block their opponents away from the play as indicated and then go through to block off the opponent's secondary defense.

No. 18—The other play in the above diagram is a fake center buck, made to look like No. 17 and is an excellent ground gainer. At the snap of the ball to No. 2, No. 4 helps block the tackle in. The right guard leaves his position and runs out to block the opponent's end out. No. 3 dives into the place left vacant by the right guard; No. 2 starts with the ball as if to hit the center, but when about a yard from the line he turns to the left and hands the ball to the left end who leaves his position at the snap of the ball and carries it just outside of the opponent's left tackle. No. 1 runs toward the position left vacant by the end to prevent anyone following and catching the runner from behind and also to add to the confusion of the opponents. This is an excellent play and works equally well with the end or tackle running with the ball.

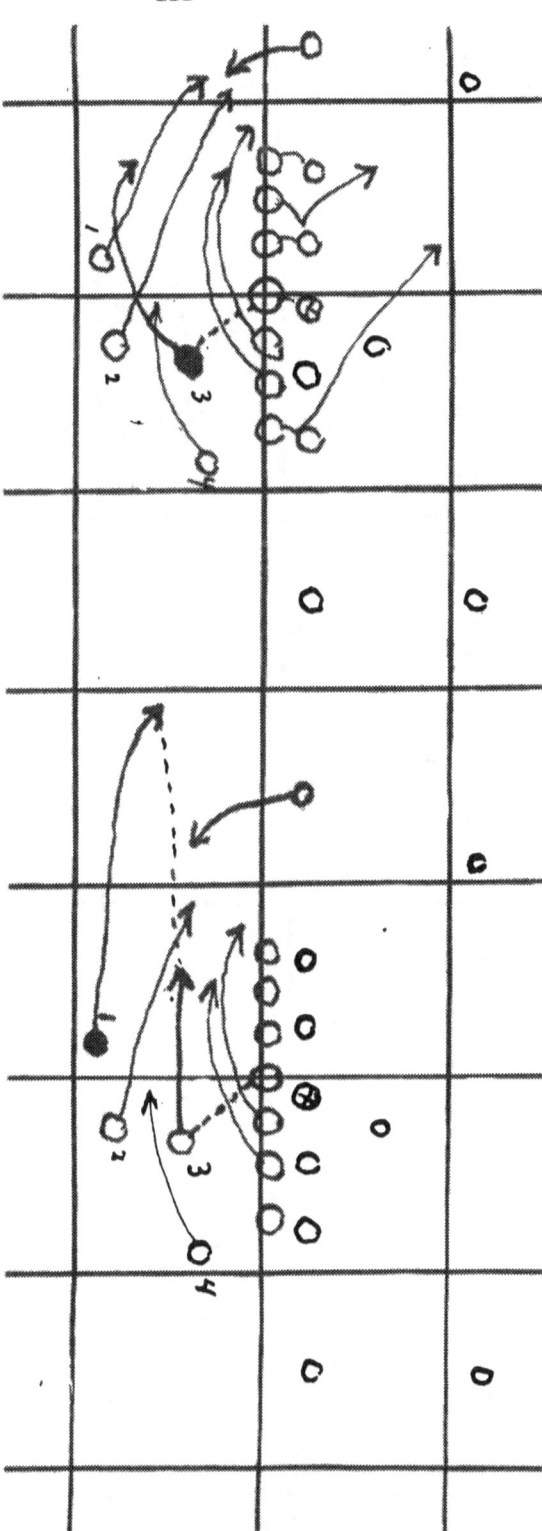

No. 19—In this play the ball is passed direct to No. 3, who starts a little back, using No. 1, No. 2 and right guard and tackle for interference, and either circles the opposing end or cuts in just outside of tackle. If the opposing end is playing wide the interference will carry him out and the runner should turn inside, but if the interference is able to box the end in then the runner makes a wide end run.

No. 20—The other play starts off just like No. 19 except that No. 1 runs straight out, and No. 3 also straight out, passing the ball to No. 1 when about to be tackled. In this play the pass cannot be a forward pass because No. 3 is within five yards of the line of scrimmage.

112

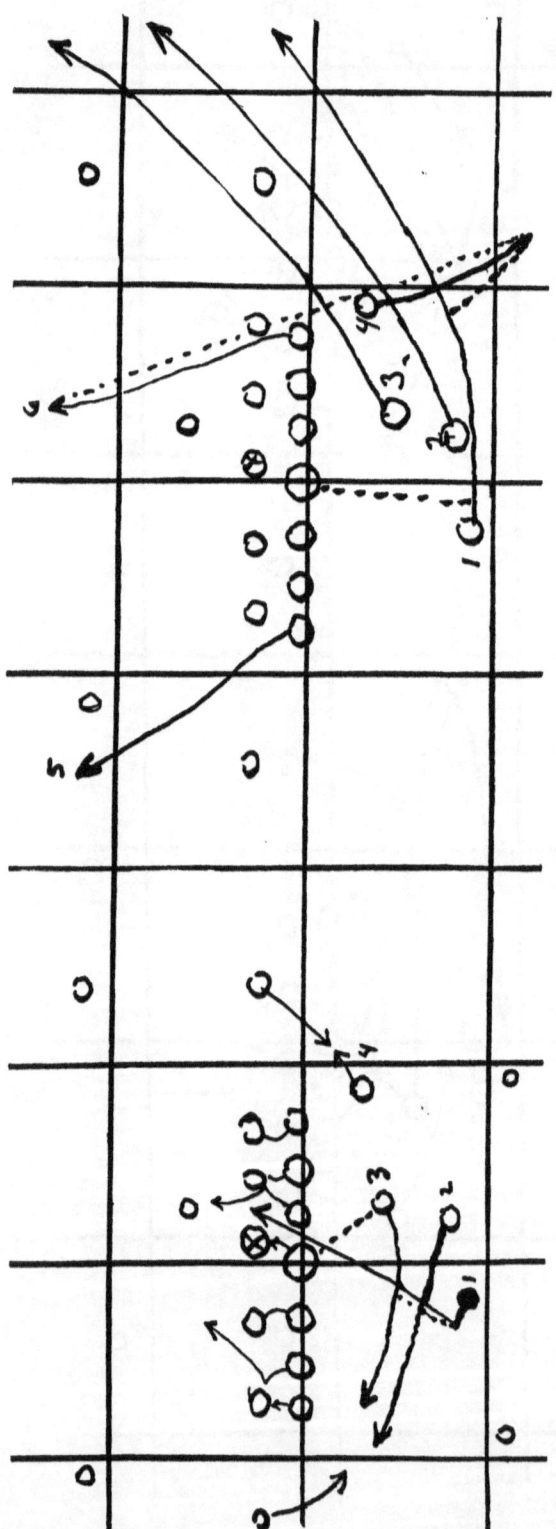

No. 21—In this play No. 3 carries the ball to the left behind No. 2 and as he passes No. 1 he hands him the ball and the latter shoots through the line as indicated. No. 1 takes one step a little forward and a little to the left and keeps close to the ground so as not to attract the attention of the opponents before he obtains the ball from No. 3. No. 4 blocks as indicated to prevent opponents from overtaking the runner from behind.

No. 22—At the snap of the ball No. 4 drops back and No. 1 starts around opponent's left end, passing the ball to No. 4 as he passes him. No. 4 must be five yards back of the line when he makes the pass. He can pass to No. 6 or No. 5, or to Nos. 1, 2, or 3. The pass to No. 6 seems to work best.

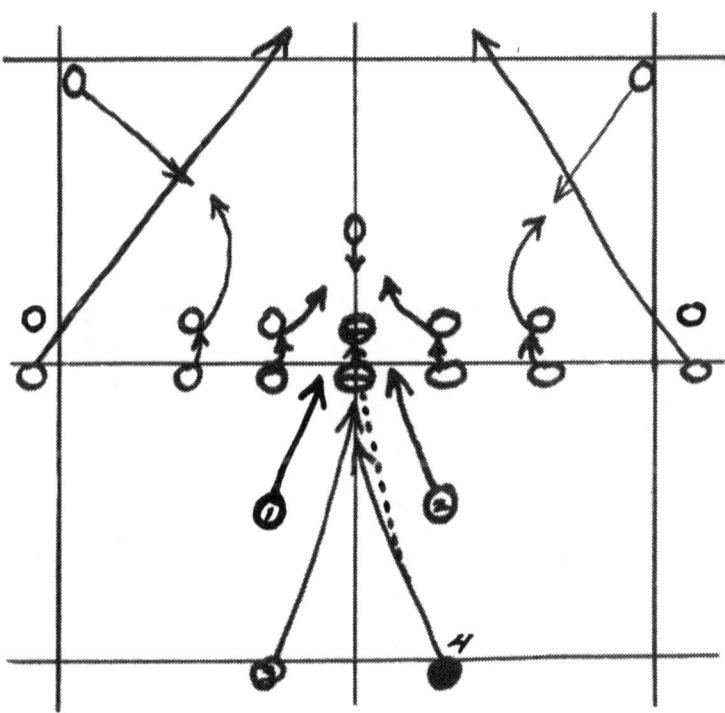

OPEN DIRECT PASS FORMATION

No. 23. This play and the following up to No. 28, are from an open formation which will prove very effective under the new rules. The linemen all play opposite their opponents and, as the defense is usually pretty well spread out, the result will be a very open formation. Two of the backs play about three yards back of the line and about three yards apart. The other two backs play about six yards from the line and the same distance apart, the four backs forming a square. In this position either of the two backs numbered 3 and 4 can attack any spot in the line with the other three backs for interference, thus forming mass plays as well as end runs without violating the rules. The open line tends to prevent congestion when the play hits the line. This play is an attack upon center which explains itself. Nos. 1, 2 and 3 interfere for No. 4. Guards and tackles block their men out and then go through and block off the secondary defense as indicated. The ends go down the field at once so as to interfere for the runner if he gets through the line.

From this information the center can pass the ball to either No. 1 or No. 2, for dashes through quick openings in the line between guard and tackle when a short gain is needed.

NOTE—Since the plays from this formation were diagramed it has been found by experience that all the plays work better by having the ends play close in by the tackles and helping the latter take care of the opposing tackles on all runs inside or outside of the latter and letting the interference take care of the ends on plays outside the tackles.

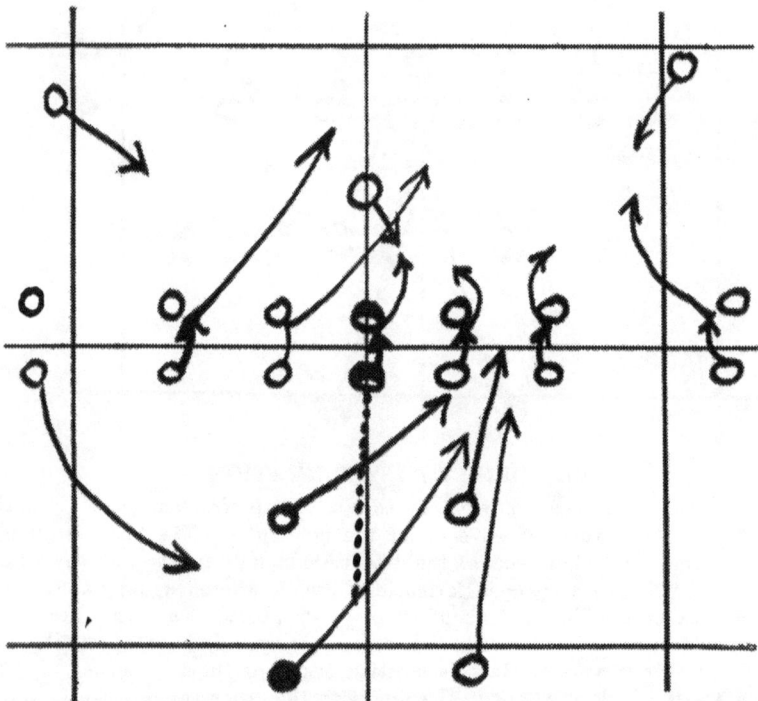

No. 24. This play is very similar to the preceding play except that it is aimed between guard and tackle. Left end comes around to guard against opponents securing the ball upon a fumble and to protect the runner from the rear.

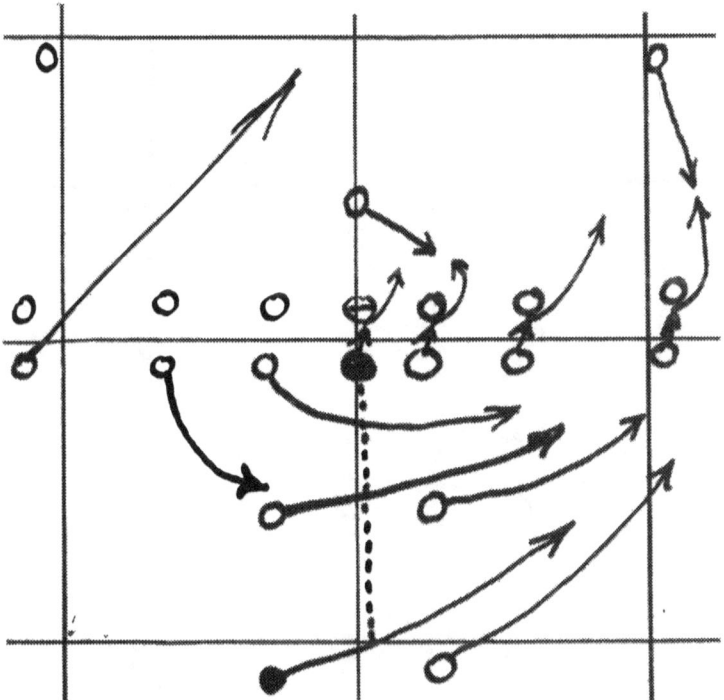

No. 25. End run. Left half takes the ball around right end, the other backs and left guard interfering for him. Left tackle follows up the play and makes it safe, while left end cuts across the field to interfere for the runner if he gets by the line. Center and the right side of the line block long and hard and then go through and cut off secondary defense.

NOTE—With the ends playing in close to the tackles left tackle gets into the interference and left end follows up the play to make it safe.

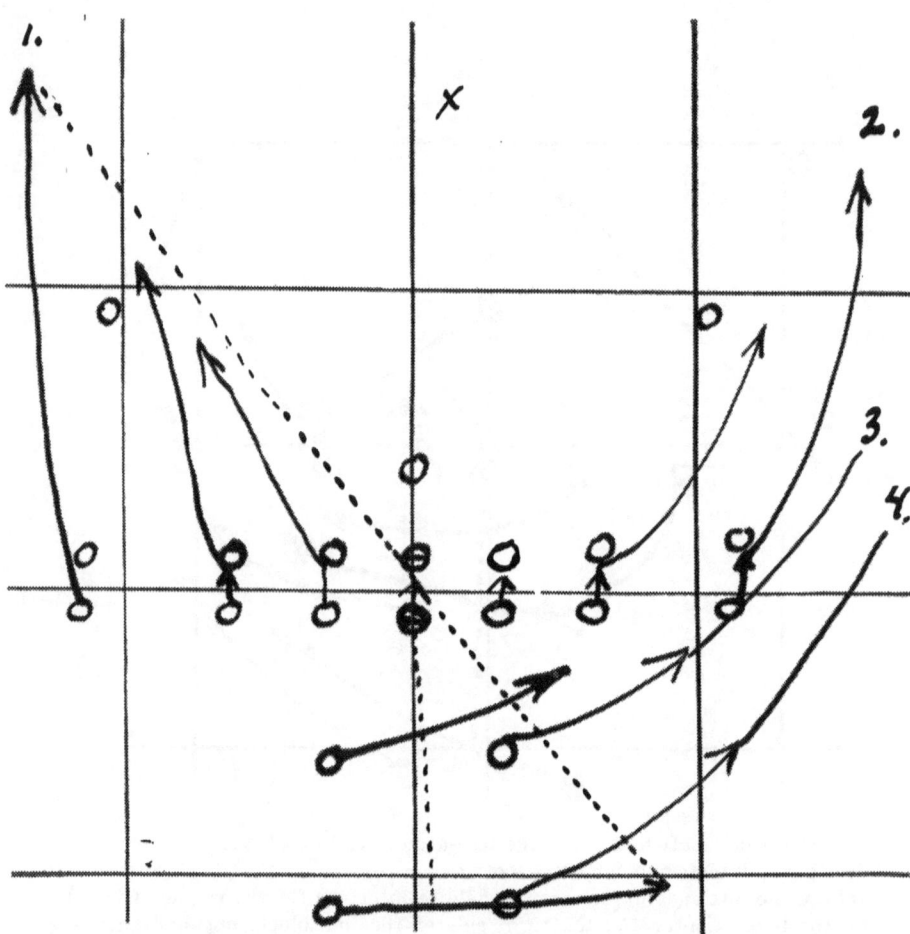

No. 26. This is a fake end run to the right and a forward pass across the line to left end marked No. 1. The play starts off like the preceding play, but left half passes the ball after running about five to seven yards, or farther if he is not interfered with. He must, of course, pass the ball before advancing within five yards of the line. He can also pass to players marked 2, 3 or 4 if left end is covered and it might be well to have right end run to the spot marked X so that the pass could be made to that spot if the others were covered.

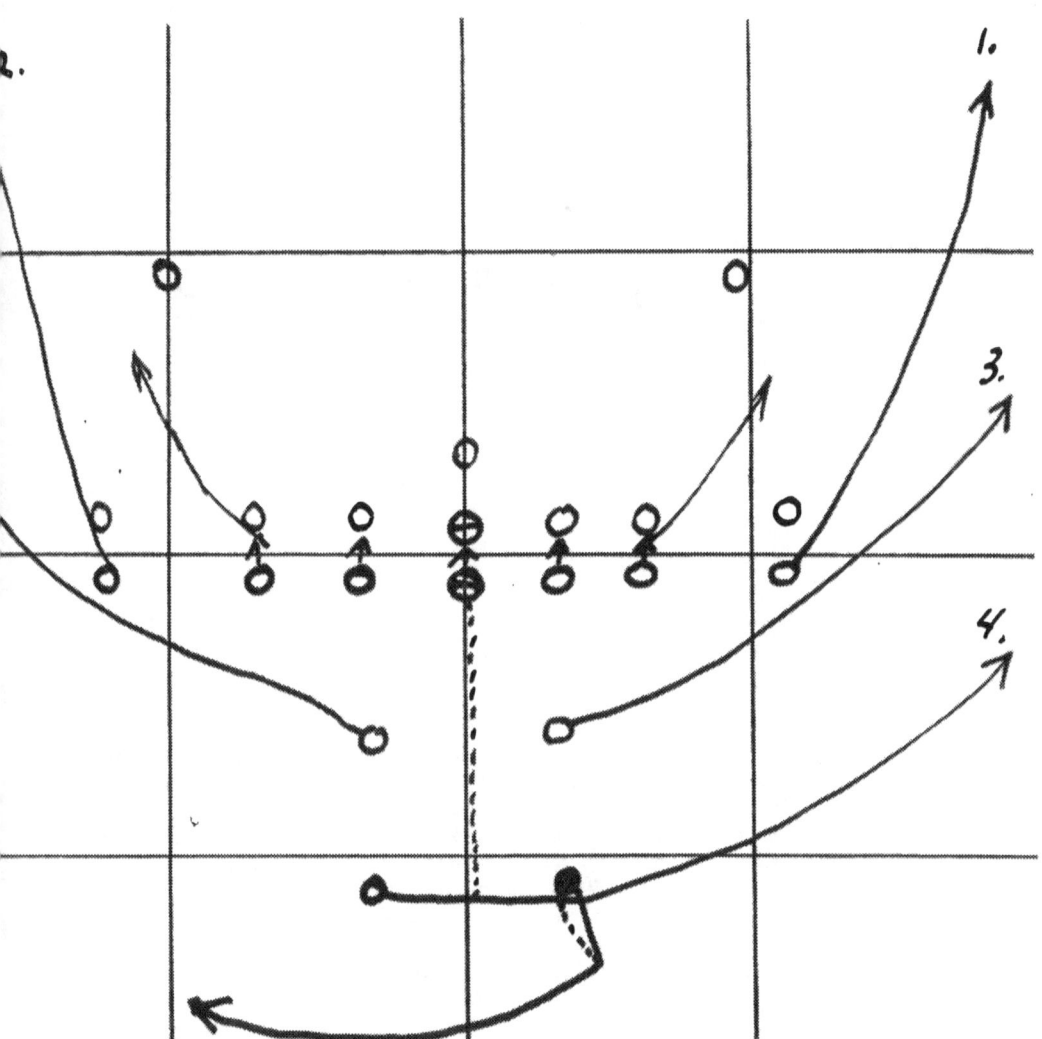

No. 27. This is a criss-cross ending in a forward pass. Left half starts to the right with the ball. Right half backs up and faces to the left and receives the ball from left half as he passes him. Right half then runs back to the left. While these maneuvers are taking place the other backs and the ends run for uncovered positions as indicated and left half continues his run to the right. Right half can now pass the ball to No. 1, 2, 3, 4 or 5 whichever is uncovered. No. 2 seems to be the most likely place to pass to. The other line men block long and hard.

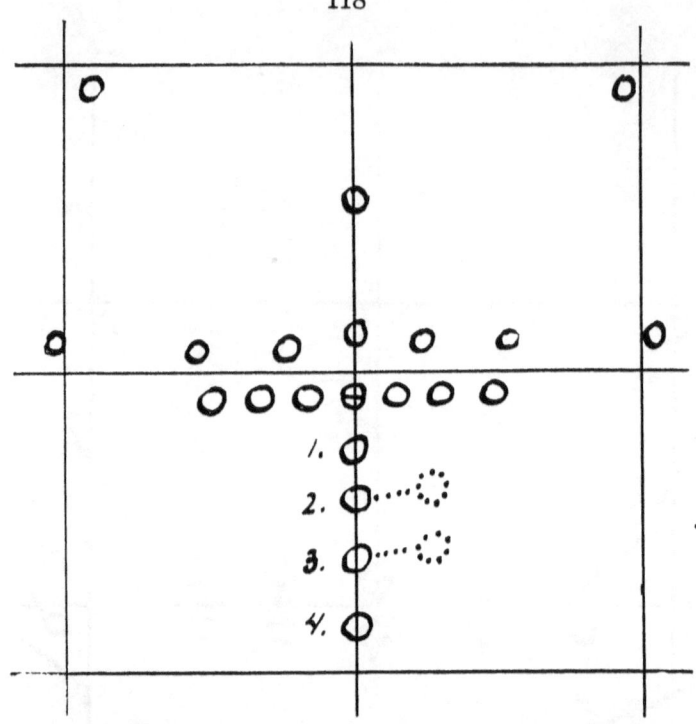

BACKS IN LINE—QUICK SHIFT FORMATION.

No. 28. The following seven diagrams explain plays from the above formation. This is a very effective quick-shift formation because the shift can be made to either side and so quickly that the opponents do not have time to shift their defense before the play starts.

The line formation is regular, but the backs line up in tandem form, directly behind center. The quarter, No. 1, is in his regular position. No. 2 should be the back who is least skillful in running with the ball but a good interferer. No. 3 should be the best line-bucking back, probably the fullback, and No. 4 should be the cleverest end running back.

With the backs standing in this tandem position the quarter gives the signal so that all the players know what the play is to be and upon which side the shift is to be made. Having given the signal the quarter can clap his hands, yell "Hike," or give any other signal which the two backs behind him can see or hear and at the signal the two backs numbered 2 and 3 jump over to the right or left and the ball is snapped to the quarter the instant the center sees the feet of players 2 and 3 hit the ground. These plays are no violation against the rule prohibiting players being in motion when the ball is put in play, because if the shift is made by a hop or jump there is a momentary stop when the feet of players 2 and 3 hit the ground and the ball is put in play at that time.

It will be advisable to have one fake signal so that the shirts may be made occasionally and the ball not be put in play, in order to prevent the oppon-

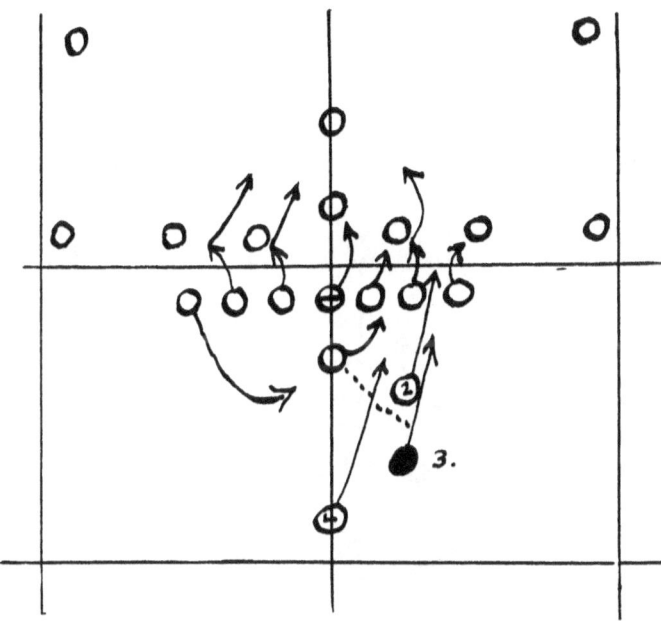

ents from charging when the shift is made. On this fake signal it should be understood that if the opponents charge when the backs shift, the center will pass the ball so as to secure a penalty for off-side play.

The following seven plays are to be played from this quick shift formation, but they can also be played without the quick shift feature and are very effective if played with or without the shift.

No. 29. This play is a straight plunge by the full-back or player No. 3 between the opponent's tackle and guard. Quarter receives the ball from center and passes it to No. 3. No. 2 goes ahead of the runner to force an opening and to block off the secondary defense players. The quarter and No. 4 rush into the line by the side of No. 3 and help bend the line back if there is no hole, and the left end comes around to look out for a fumble. The linemen block as indicated and then go through to block off the secondary defense players.

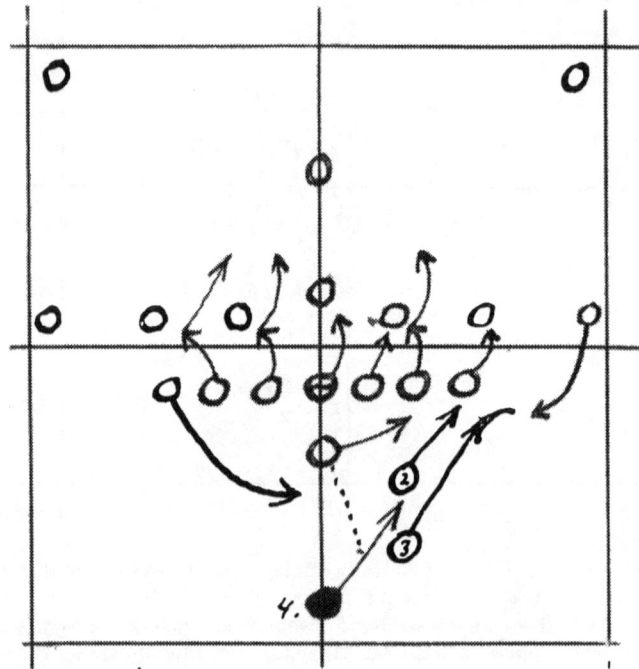

No. 30. Mass on tackle or off-tackle play. Quarter passes the ball to No. 4, who runs behind No. 2 straight at or a bit outside of the opposing left tackle. No. 3 runs at his side and dives into the end when that player comes in to tackle the runner. The quarter runs at the inside of No. 4 and protects him from that side. Left end comes around to make the play safe and the linemen block as indicated in the diagram.

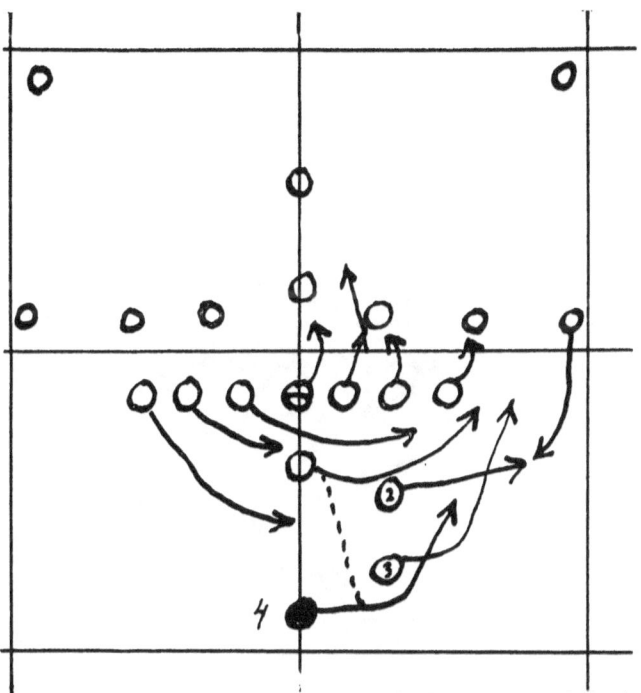

No. 31. This is a very effective run outside of tackle considerably wider than the preceding play. The play should start off as for a wide end run, but the interference and the man with the ball should turn in quickly after taking about three steps to the right. No. 2 blocks the end out and No .3 should turn in quickly just as No. 2 blocks the end. No. 4 should follow No. 3. The latter should help No. 2 block the end if necessary. The quarter and left guard and tackle should come around quickly and form interference, turning in quickly just outside their own right end. Left end follows the play to make it safe.

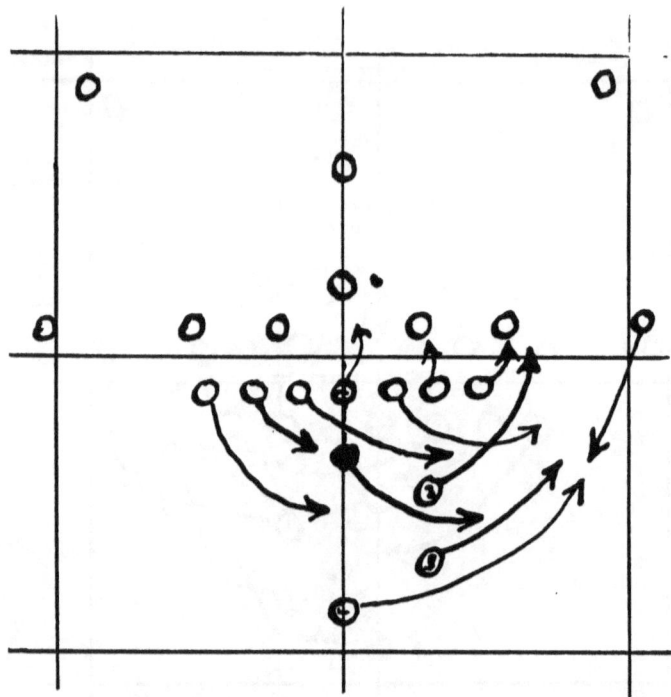

No. 32. This is a wide quarter-back run. No. 2 helps block the opponent's left tackle and No. 3 and No. 4 should block the end in and both guards and left tackle should get into the interference, left end following the runner from behind. The quarter should start well back and then turn in when he sees an opening.

123

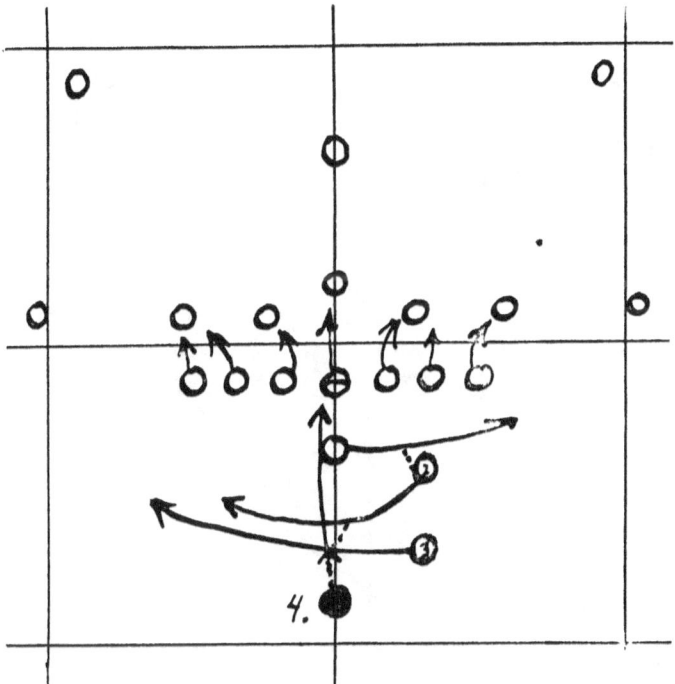

No. 33. This is a tripple pass delayed center buck and will be found very effective if the ball is handled properly. The quarter gets the ball from center and runs to the right, handing it to No. 2 as he passes him. No. 2 then starts a little back to the left behind No. 3 who preceeds him and as he passes No. 4 he hands him the ball for a plunge straight through center. In this play the quarter and No. 3 start when the ball is put in play but No. 2 and No. 4 do not start until they get the ball. No. 4 can move up a bit closer to the line after No. 3 passes in front of him.

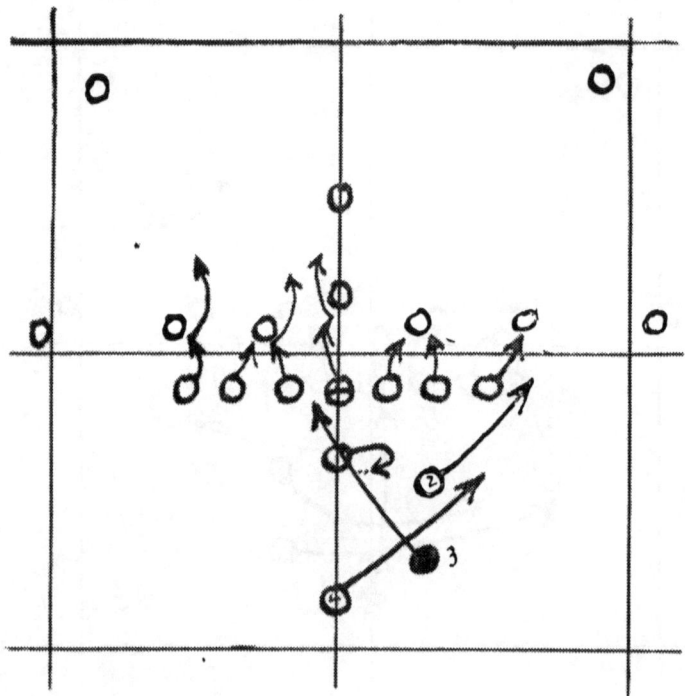

No. 34. This is an effective fake or split play. The play is made to look like No. 28. The quarter turns to the right and makes a bluff to pass the ball to No. 4 for a tackle play but continues to turn around and after No. 4 has passed, the quarter, with his back to the line, passes the ball to No. 3 who has stood still. The latter plunges through the line on the left side, center and left guard making an opening for him and the other linemen blocking as indicated.

125

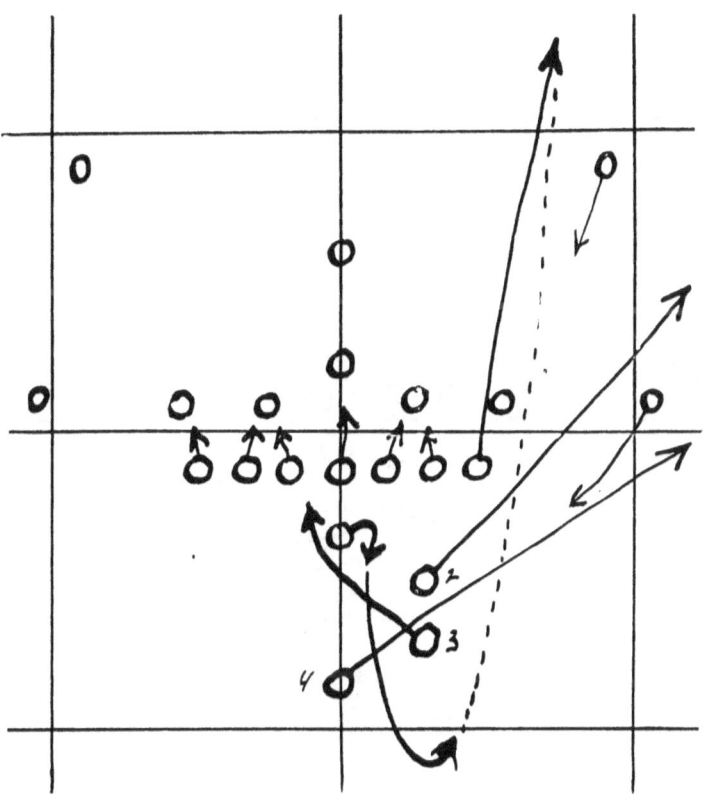

No. 35. This is a forward pass play which starts off exactly as the preceeding play, but the quarter after making a bluff to pass the ball to No. 4 and then to No. 3, runs with it himself well back and to the right, passing it forward to the right end or to players No. 2 or No. 4. This is an effective forward pass because it is delayed and the players who may receive it have plenty of time to get into uncovered positions.

NOTE.—From this formation other simple and effective plays can be added, such as the quarter diving straight through center with the ball or passing it to No. 2 for a quick plunge through either side of guard.

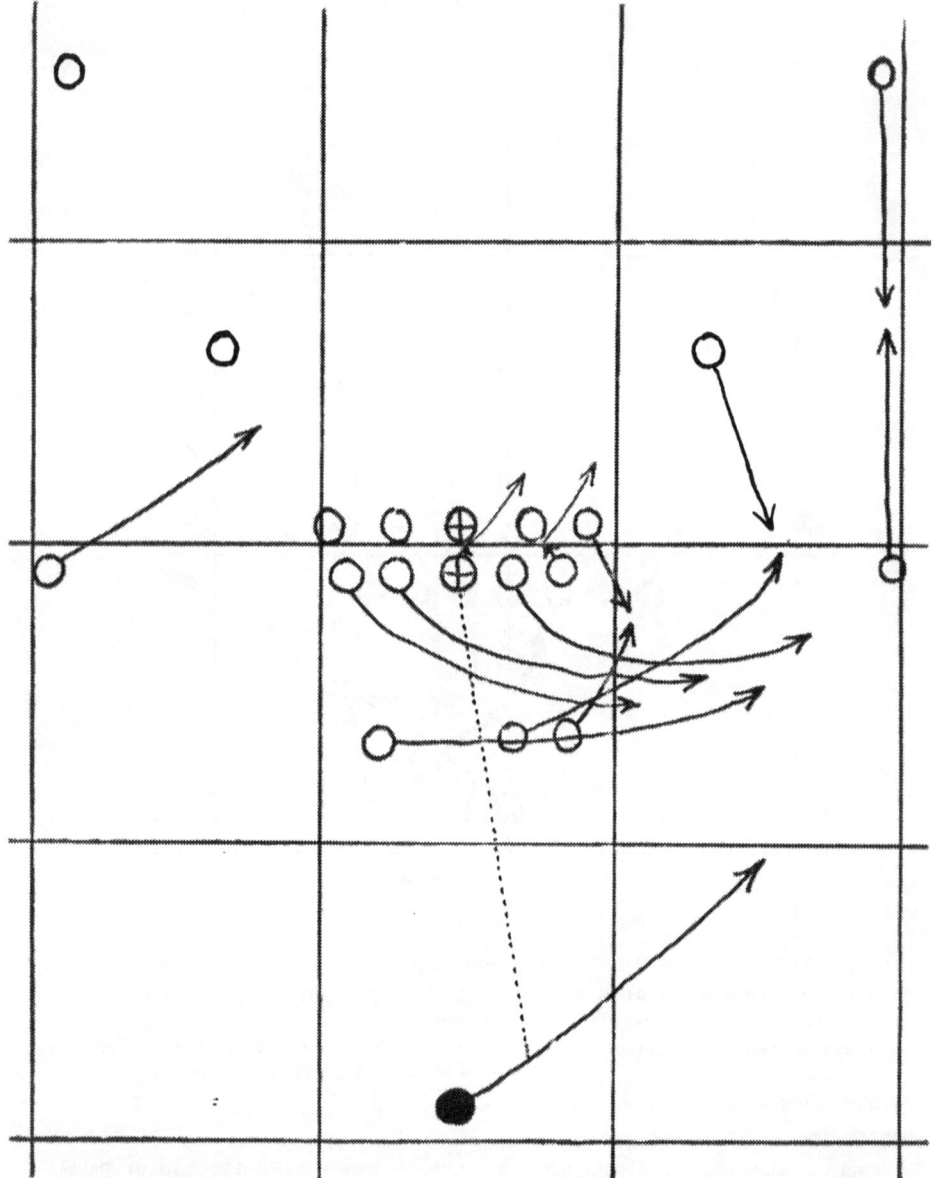

No. 36. This and the following plays are from the punt formation. The center passes the ball to the right, the punter receiving it upon the run. The line men and backs block or interfere as indicated. Speed is a great factor in this play. Note that the right guard gets into the interference, and that right half blocks the opposing tackle.

From this information most of the punting should be done, it not being considered necessary to diagram the punt play, as the duties of the players are either apparent or are explained elsewhere in the book.

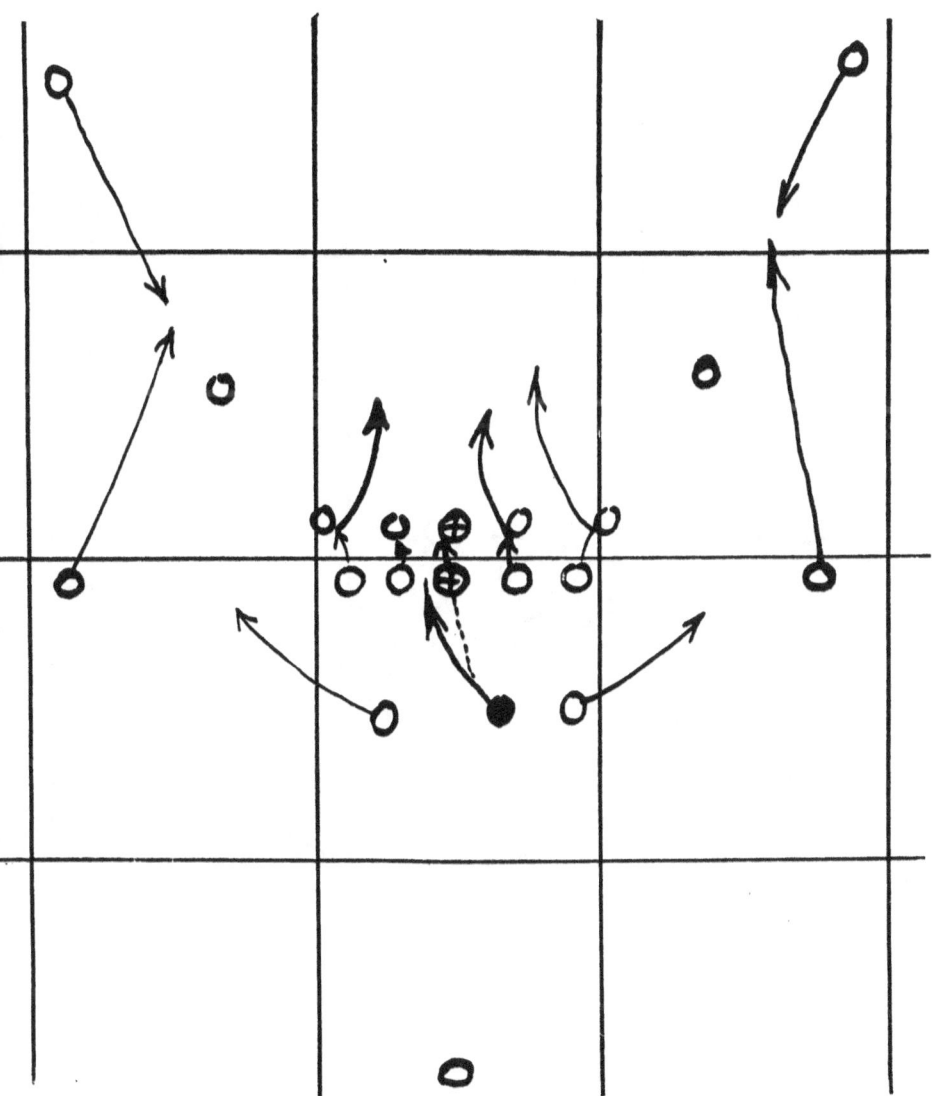

No. 38. Direct pass to back indicated who darts through quick opening made by left guard and center. The other backs run out to help draw attention away from the play. The other linemen push their opponents out and go through to block off the secondary defense.

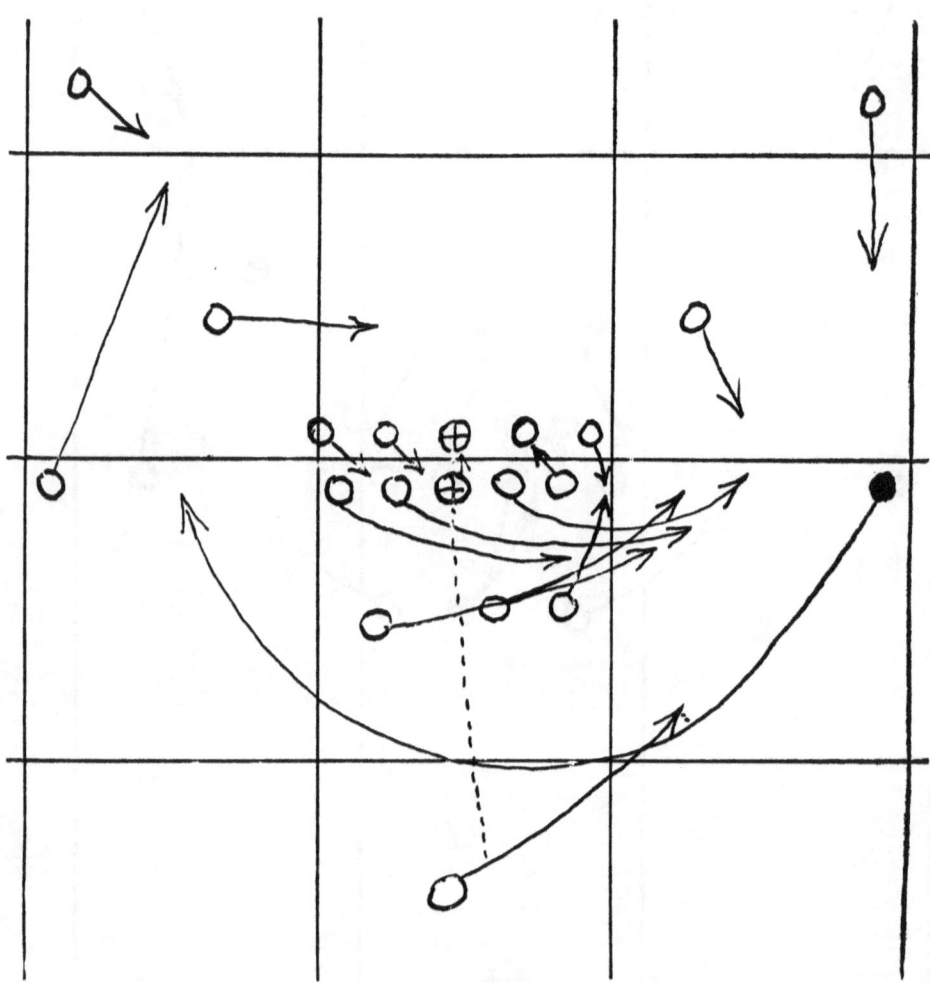

No. 37. This play starts off like No. 36, but the man receiving the ball passes it to right end, who leaves his position with the snap of the ball and swings around the opposite end. This is a criss-cross that works.

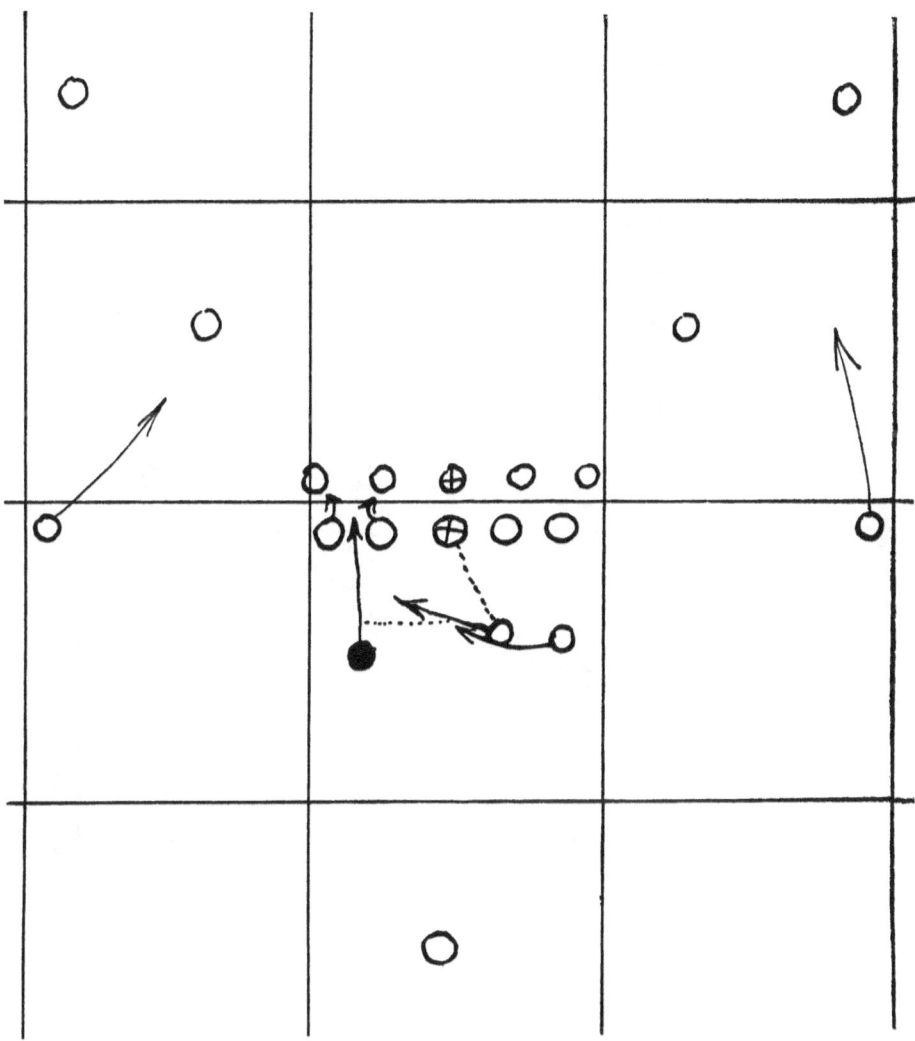

No. 39. Fake kick. The ball is passed to quarter and he passes it across to left half, who darts through the line between guard and tackle. Quarter and right half go into the line by the side of the runner to help bend the line back in case left guard and tackle are unable to make an opening.

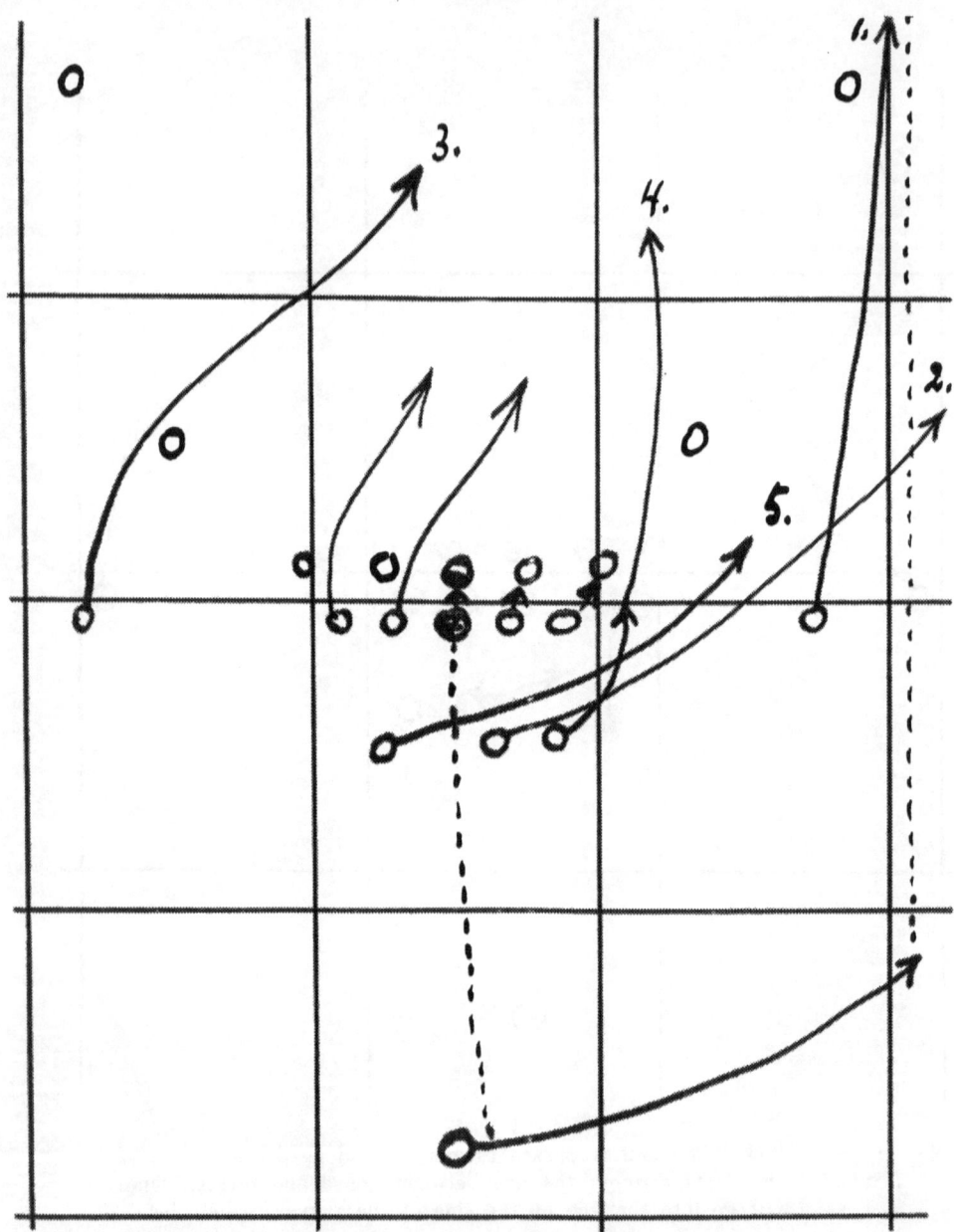

No. 40. Forward pass after a run to the right. The play is made to look like play No. 21 and the two are used to help each other and keep the opponents guessing. The player who stands back apparently for a punt secures the ball on the run from center and places it under his right arm so as to make the opponents think he intends to circle the end. When he has run well out he passes the ball either to No. 1 or to No. 2, but he can also pass to No. 3 or 4 if the others are covered. The pass to No. 1 or No. 2 will probably prove the best play.

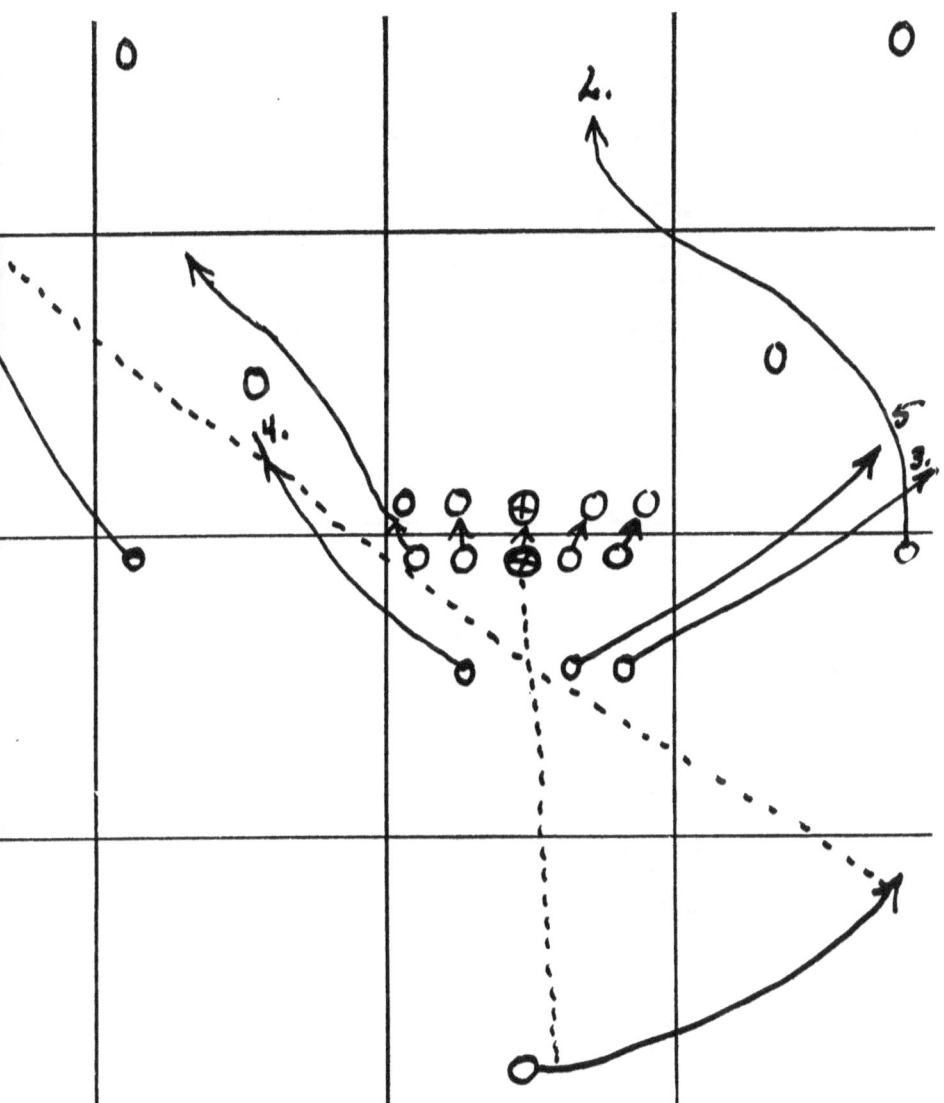

No. 41. Run to the right with a pass back across to the left end. The pass will probably work best to No. 1, but if this player is covered the pass can be made to No. 2 who should be ready to receive it. Nos. 3, 4 and 5 run as indicated so as to draw some of the defense to cover them and leave No. 1 and No. 2 uncovered.

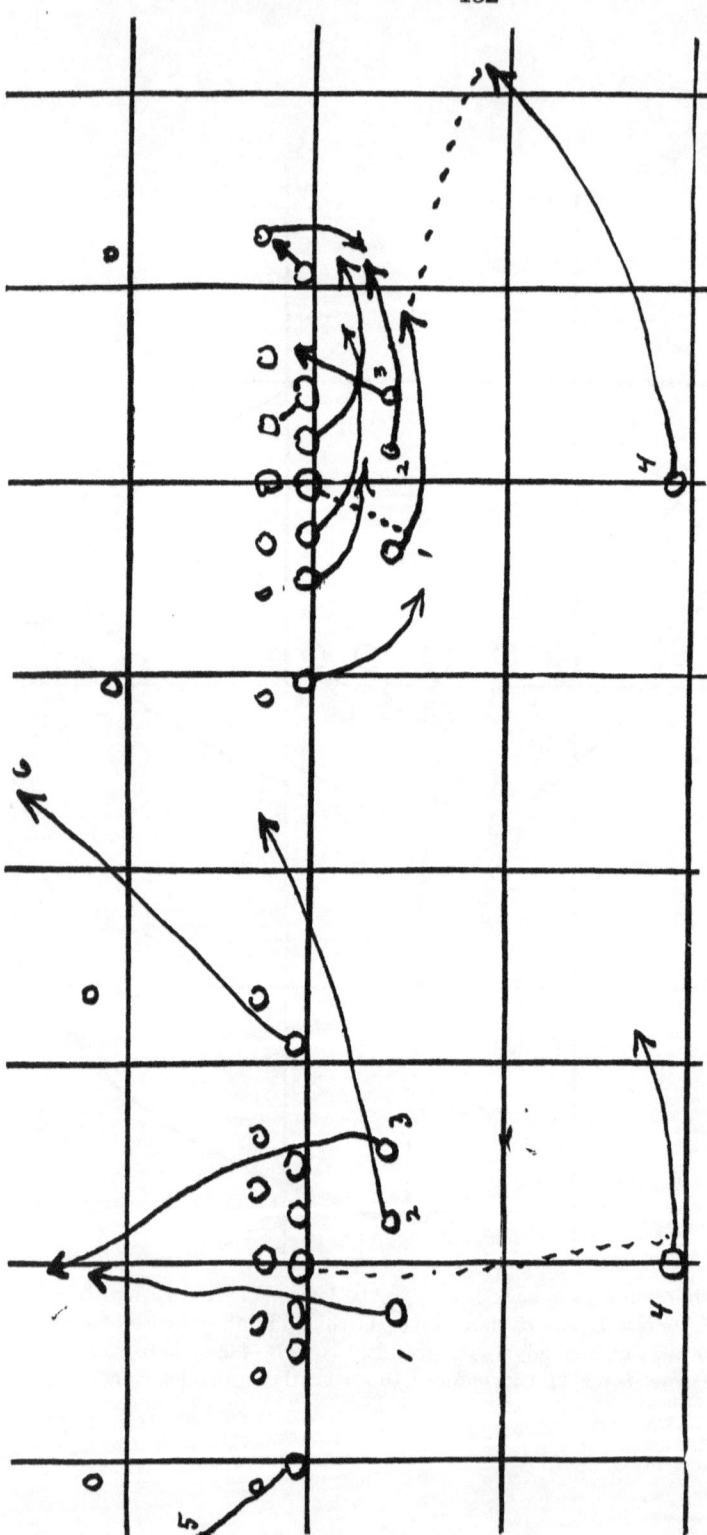

No. 42—No. 4 plays back ten yards. At the snap of the ball No. 1 and No. 3 run to a point directly in front of where the ball was put in play. No. 6 and No. 5 run well down the field and a little out. No. 2 runs well out to the side and just across the scrimmage line. No. 4 starts to the right and then passes to No. 1 and No. 2, or to No. 2, 6, or 5. The pass to Nos. 1 and 3, or to No. 2 works best. No. 1 and No. 3 should aim to be at the same spot so that if one of them should happen to be blocked off and prevented from getting into position the other will be there. It is not likely that both will be unable to get into position.

No. 43—In this play No. 1 gets the ball from center and after running as far as he can he passes to No. 4. The other players block, or form interference as indicated.

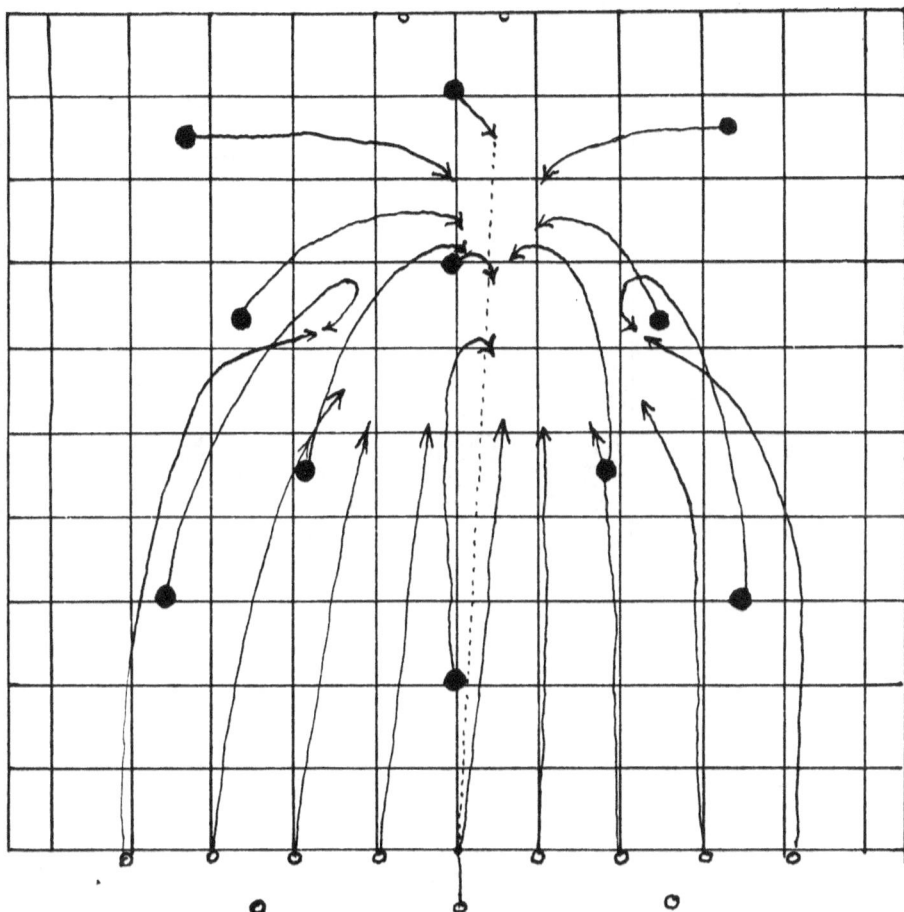

No. 44. This diagram explains a good formation and interference for running back kick-offs and kick-outs from the twenty yard line, and place kicks (after fair catches) which do not score or result in touchdowns.

The ends should be fifteen yards from the side line, so as to guard against short kicks to the side. Center stands ten yards from the ball, also to guard against a short kick. The diagram shows positions of all. The distance the backs should stand from the ball depends upon the wind, and upon the ability of the kicker. The whole team should run back toward the spot where the ball is to be caught, and turn in time to block opponents and form fast and close interference for the runner. The ends should keep on the inside of their opponents, and block them out as they turn in to tackle the runner. In fact all the men should endeavor to block their opponents out. Center should dodge the ball if kicked low, because if it hits him his opponents are more likely to get it than he.

On kick-outs the formation is the same, except that center stands on the twenty yard line and tries to block the kick.

NOTE.—The diagram was drawn before the rule was made that the kick-off shall be from the forty-yard line but the relative positions of the players will remain the same, the bottom line representing the forty-yard line instead of the center of the field.

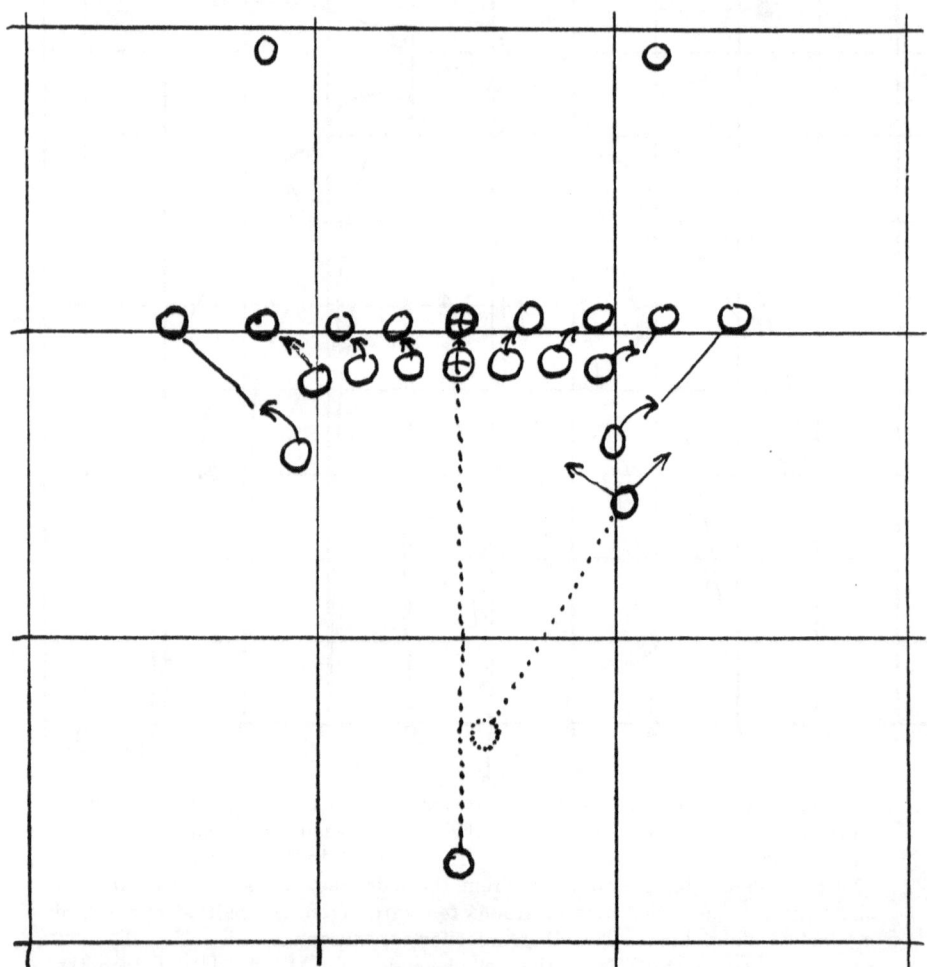

No. 45. Drop-kick or quick place-kick formation. Solid circles show formation for a drop-kick, and the dotted circle shows the holder of the ball and where he should be, in case the trial is to be by a quick place-kick. Every man who is protecting the kicker (excepting the center) should make it a point to block his man outward, so that if his opponent breaks through it will be difficult for him to get in front of the ball. In case of the drop-kick, the extra back on the right should watch for and block any man coming through the center .

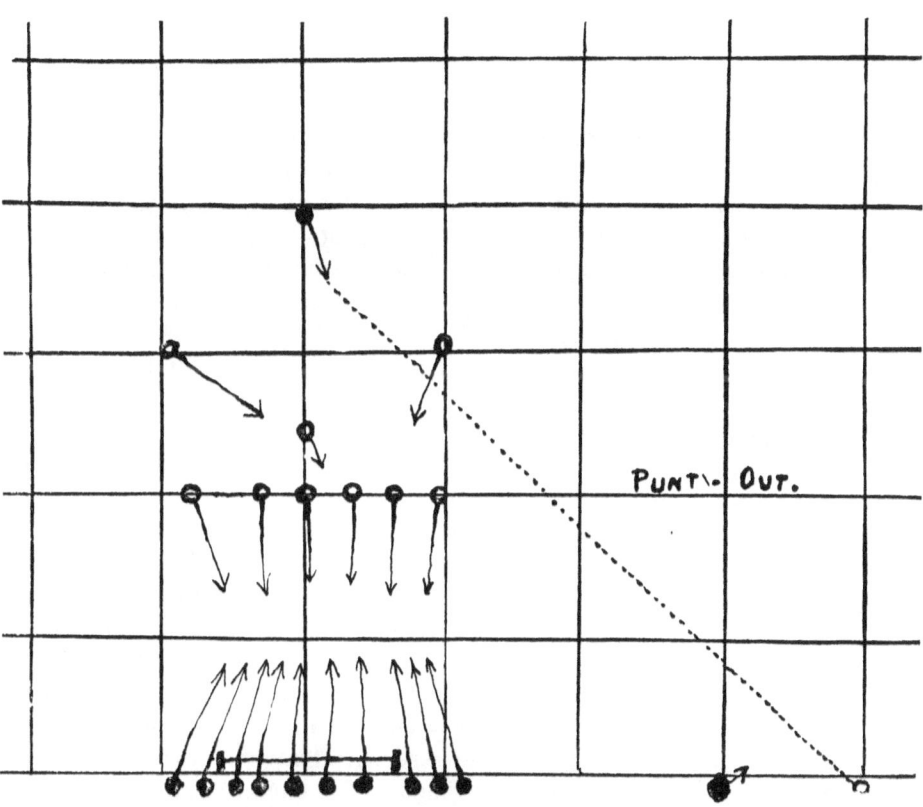

Punt-out.—A punt-out should be made after a touchdown in case the ball is declared dead more than ten yards to either side of the goal, and the diagram shows how the two teams should line up, although the line men of the side making the punt-out usually stand upon the five-yard line instead of the ten-yard line. There should be four of the best punt catchers of the punter's side stationed so as to cover the ground where the punt is likely to fall, and when one of them is sure he can catch the ball he should yell "I have it," and all the rest of his team should advance toward the opponents, so as to block them and protect the catcher.

Defense.

THERE are several different systems of defense made use of by the leading teams of the country, and all of them work fairly well when well executed. Before the changes in the rules which made the distance to be gained in three downs ten yards instead of five, and legalized forward passing, the various systems of defense used by the best teams has been thoroughly perfected, and their differences were marked and easily defined. Since the game has changed, however, changes were made necessary in these systems and a great deal of experimenting has been done for the purpose of determining what arrangement of the players, especially the defensive backs, will produce the strongest and best conceived defense for the new plays, and at the same time successfully guard against the old ones.

The problem which has to be solved is to arrange the players so as to guard the territory lying between the scrimmage line and the territory about twenty-five yards back of it, which is guarded by the defensive back, who always plays back for punts. If unguarded, forward passes can be placed from five to twenty yards beyond the scrimmage line and recovered by the team making them, and thus thwart the strongest possible defense for ordinary running plays. On the other hand, if too many men are withdrawn from a position near the line of scrimmage, and stationed so far back to guard against forward passes that they cannot properly aid in stopping the regular running plays, the latter can easily be made to gain consistently.

The arrangement of the defensive backs, used by many of the leading teams, has been to place one player about ten or fifteen yards back of the scrimmage line, whose primary duty is to guard against forward passes, another about twenty-five or thirty yards back to guard against punts the same as formerly, leaving the other two about three or four yards back of the two tackles to back up the line and guard against the regular running plays. In addition to this, the men in the line have been played a little farther apart, in order to be in a better position to guard against plays outside of tackle, under the assumption that such plays will be relied upon more by the team in possession of the ball than plays through the line.

Under this system of defense, the players of course shift where the opponents present a one-sided formation. The ends usually play from three to five yards out, and are supposed to watch for forward passes and aid in stopping them, as well as to guard against running plays outside of tackle, and trick plays.

While this system of defense was used by more teams than any other system since the forward pass became legalized, I think it was for the reason that one or two of the leading teams started it, and the others followed, and not because it has been demonstrated that it was best. I believe that time and experience will prove that one man, placed ten or fifteen yards back of the scrimmage line, will not be able to successfully guard against forward passes. The very nature of these plays makes them more successful when placed well to the side, and as forward passing is more fully developed it will be comparatively easy to place the ball out of reach of the one man who is assigned the difficult task of guarding the territory extending fifteen to twenty yards to either side of him .

It will prove to be a better arrangement of the defensive backs, if they are so placed that forward passes are guarded against by a half-back on each side, playing about two to four yards outside the tackles, and about five yards back of the scrimmage line, leaving one back (the full back) whose sole duty it is (with the aid of the center when the center is playing back of the line) to back up the line, and aid in stopping all running plays. The quarter-back, of course, plays in the extreme backfield to guard against punts and long forward passes, as in other systems. Under this system of defense, the half-backs are not only stationed in a favorable position to diagnose and spoil forward passes, but they are admirably situated for stopping end runs and plays outside of tackle, and the whole line can be played closer together, so that with only one man to back it up, it will be able to prevent the opponents from making consistent gains by line attacks. With this arrangement of the backs, the ends can play close in, and go into every play more recklessly, because they need not be on the alert for side kicks and passes, and the half-backs need not be so far away that they cannot aid materially in stopping plays aimed at the line.

Under the present rules, any system of defense will have to be an elastic one, changing under different weather conditions, and according to the position of the ball on the field, the number of the down, and the distance to be gained, and the defensive backs must necessarily use their heads a great deal more than was necessary a few years ago. They should be able to judge accurately what sort of tactics will be used upon each play, closing in when they are reasonably sure that no forward pass or kick will be attempted, and moving back under circumstances where it is quite probable that such plays will be resorted to.

The changes in the rules in recent years have not made it necessary to change the schemes of line defense so much as the back-field defense, and consequently there has been little modification of the duties of the center, guards, tackles, and ends, although under some systems the latter are expected to aid in stopping forward pass plays, and many teams play their centers back of the line to aid the fullback in backing up the line and heading off all plays outside of tackles. There has also been a tendency to play the guards, tackles, and ends a little farther apart than in former years when mass plays aimed at the line were used so much.

Under the first system of back-field defense described, where only one man is played several yards back, to guard against onside kicks and forward passes, the ends are usually played farther out than under the other system, since they are supposed to aid in those plays, but under the other system, where the half-backs are played rather wide, the ends are usually played closer to the tackles, because they need not bother about short kicks and forward passes, nor be so careful about a play getting around them, the backs being in such a favorable position for stopping them. It has never been definitely proven whether the ends can render better service upon the defense by playing reasonably wide, or by playing close to the tackle. Some prominent teams have been in the habit of playing their ends about five yards outside of tackle, and their defensive playing has been good; other prominent teams have been accustomed to playing their ends very close to the tackles, and this method of end defense has proved successful; but a majority of teams have adopted a middle course, neither placing the ends very wide nor very close in, but stationing them about three yards from the tackles, and this plan has worked well. As a matter of fact, the distance away from a tackle which an end should play upon defense depends entirely upon the tactics he employs in playing his position, and where he can play the better. Some ends will naturally play better by being out some distance, while others can accomplish more by playing close in, and therefore it would seem the best plan not to have any hard-and-fast rule on any team, but to let the ends play in the position and in the manner best suited to each individual, so long as they do not go to extremes. Upon the Carlisle team in 1907, Gardner played defensive end about five yards out, while Exendine, the other end, played almost within an arm's length of his tackle, and both rendered excellent service. It is probable that if the former had been coached to play close to the tackle, and the other out several yards, it would have spoiled the defensive playing of both.

It is now quite generally recognized that the guards and tackles should always charge through when upon the defense, and never run back behind their own line; but the centers of many teams are coached to play a little back from the scrimmage line, and not so low as the guards and tackles, in which position they watch the backs as well as the ball, and head off the plays in every direction; by leaving their position and running behind their own line when the play is not aimed at them. This is varied by occasionally charging through with the snap of the ball, or pushing the opposing center back into the quarter-back or the play. This seems to be the most generally used and most effective method of playing center under the present rules because there are not so many line plays as formerly and because the defensive backs have to play back so far to be upon the lookout for forward passes and short kicks. When the opponents have but a short distance to gain for a first down and are likely to try to gain the distance by a line play the center should play in the line and the backs move up a little closer to the line.

The defense for a punt or the punt formation is usually planned in the following manner: The ends drop back about four or five yards, and about the same distance outside the tackles. Two backs drop back about five to seven yards back and outside of the ends, moving out farther if the opposing ends play wide so as to be in a position to cover them. The center, guards and tackles should play higher—not having either hand upon the ground, because in this position they are more shifty upon their feet, can use their hands better in breaking through, and when through will be in an erect position ready to block the kick. The two best punt-catching backs are stationed about thirty yards back of the line, and about twenty yards apart, so that one of them will be sure to be able to get under the punt, while the other protects him and looks out for a fumble. If the center plays back and backs up the line on the ordinary defense he should also play back upon the punt formation and look out for fakes through the line, head off end runs, etc.

The two backs first mentioned, and the ends, watch the ball until sure it is to be punted, and then, if there is no fake, follow the opposing ends down the field, keeping on the inside and blocking them as they slow up preparatory to the tackle.

The ends and backs should not run back until assured that no fake is intended, and when they see that the play is going to be an attempt to rush the ball instead of a punt or a forward pass, they should rush up and head off the play.

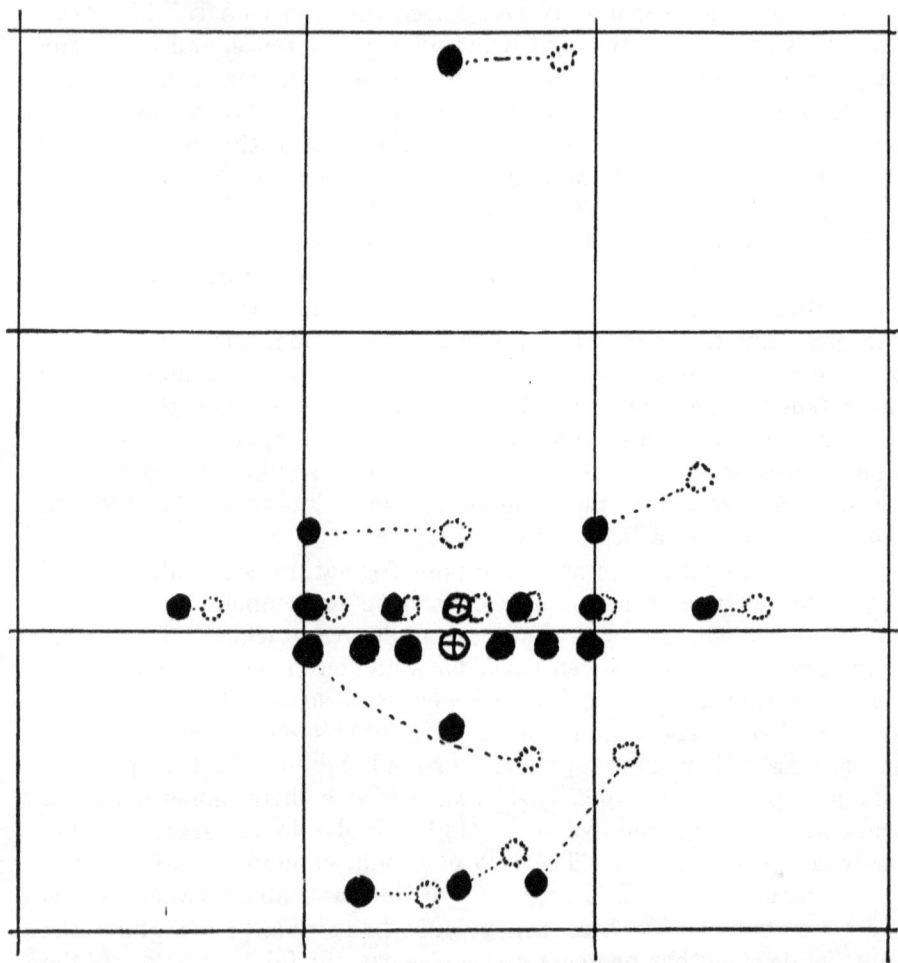

This system of defense for the punt formation should be varied occasionally by the ends playing upon the line, and attempting to block the kick. It is especially advisable to do this when the opponents are punting from a position near their own goal, because a blocked kick usually results in a touchdown here, and the punter is usually a bit nervous and will not be able to punt so well with so many rushing at him and hurrying him, and besides these reasons, it is very likely that the defending backfield players will attempt a fair catch, and in that case it is not necessary that the opposing ends should be blocked. Many teams play their ends upon the line all the time in defending the punt formation, depending upon the backs alone to guard against forward passes and to form interference for the man who handles the punt.

The defense for the foward pass from the punt formation need not differ materially from the defense for a punt. The defending backs should cover the ends and the defensive ends should cover the backs on their side who start down the field to get into a favorable position for receiving the pass. (This is assuming that the ends drop back on the punt formation) while the five center men go through to hurry or block the pass. If the ends play on the line in defending the punt formation they rush in to hurry or block the pass or punt, or tackle the runner if an end run is attempted.

The diagram upon the preceding page shows the system of defense first described, the solid black spots showing a regular formation and the defense for same, while the dotted circles and lines show how to form for a one-sided formation and how the defense should shift to meet it. If the team having the ball should have still more strength upon one side of the ball, the defense should shift farther, always keeping a well-balanced defense in front of the other team, no matter where the ball is situated. In the diagram the quarter-back, or the extreme back field player, is not shown, there not being room on the diagram.

On the opposite or following page is shown a photograph of the best and most generally used defense.

142

The above illustration shows the second defensive formation previously described, which I believe will be found to be the most satisfactory, and come into more general use. The positions to be assumed for this system of defense are also shown in the diagrams of plays under the head of Offense, the regular defense being opposed to regular formation plays, and a shifted defense being shown in position for defending one-sided formations. In this illustration the defensive center is playing upon the line, some of the best teams play the center back of the line just in front of the defensive fullback and other teams play the center and full-back side by side, one about three yards behind each guard.

The positions for the defense of the punt formation are also shown in the diagrams of plays from this formation, the center often playing back about four yards instead of on the line.

As has been previously mentioned, the above defensive formation needs to be varied greatly under the different conditions which must be confronted during a game. When the defending team is near its own goal, the man playing the defensive position called full-back (usually the quarter-back) should move up and assist in backing up the line, because no long punt or pass can be used under such conditions. When near the side line, the defensive back upon that side can close in and assist in backing up the line, because the side line prevents any pass or side kick to that side. However, these are but variations of the above defensive formation which a little headwork or common sense should suggest to the players when such situations or conditions present themselves.

Reprints of the Pop Warner Single-Wing Trilogy

A Course in Football for Players and Coaches: Offense
Reprints of the 1908 offense pamphlet, 1909 supplement & 1910 revision from Warner's groundbreaking correspondence course on the rudiments of football. Also includes Tom Benjey's interpretation of the birth and early evolution of the singlewing offense.
ISBN-10 0-9774486-5-7
ISBN-13 978-0-9774486-5-4

A Course in Football for Players and Coaches
Reprint of Warner's 1912 hardbound version of his correspondence course on the rudiments of football. Includes an early evolution of the single-wing offense.
ISBN-10 0-9774486-6-5
ISBN-13 978-0-9774486-6-1

Football for Coaches and Players
Reprint of Warner's 1927 hardbound classic on the rudiments of football. Includes evolved unbalanced-line single-wing and double-wing formations.
ISBN-10 0-9774486-4-9
ISBN-13 978-0-9774486-4-7

Watch Carlisle Indian School football stars tackle bootleggers, socialites, the government, students and other demons while creating the professional game in Tom Benjey's upcoming book.

Tuxedo Press
546 E Springville Rd
Carlisle, PA 17015
717-258-9733
www.LoneStarDietz.com

www.ingramcontent.com/pod-product-compliance
Lightning Source LLC
Chambersburg PA
CBHW031252290426
44109CB00012B/546